Village Assignment

Dave Huebsch

Highlight Publishing
Little Falls MN

Ellen Knudsen

Village Assignment, True stories of humor adventure and drama in
Guatemala's highland villages.

Copyright © 2004 by Dave Huebsch

Published in the United States by Highlight Publishing, PO Box 27, Little
Falls, MN 56345, toll free (866) 336-6681, www.HighlightPublishing.com

ISBN 0-9741734-0-1

Library of Congress Control Number: 2003-107380

Manufactured in the United States of America

Printed by Park Press , Inc.
Waite Park, MN 56387

Village Assignment is a warm and insightful series of true stories and encounters with the villagers in the Guatemalan highlands. These episodes give the reader an insider's view of the lifestyle, difficulties, and efforts of human development workers, as well as the struggles of impoverished villagers.

Let **Village Assignment** transport you to many remote mountain villages, and give you the sense of a hands-on experience of the work, and of the people who live there.

About the author:

Dave Huebsch is a native Minnesotan, a veteran High School Language Arts Teacher, and human development worker. He continues to be in demand as a passionate speaker and homilist. He has been featured on numerous radio talk shows, and has delivered keynote addresses at National conventions. Dave Huebsch is the founder of *Common Hope* (www.CommonHope.org), which does human development in many villages in Guatemala. In 1984 he left a successful business and career in education to apply his skills in Guatemala's highland villages, which he considers his most important personal assignment.

—- Table of Contents —-

Chapter	1	An Original Child	13
Chapter	2	Life is too Fragile	18
Chapter	3	Street Magic	21
Chapter	4	The Boy and the Soldiers	25
Chapter	5	The Widow's Chickens	28
Chapter	6	Orphanage Repairs	32
Chapter	7	Women vs. Builders	35
Chapter	8	White Door-Cross	38
Chapter	9	Chiseled School	41
Chapter	10	A Shattered Roof	45
Chapter	11	The Turtle Shell	48
Chapter	12	Baskets of Plenty	51
Chapter	13	Electrical Hot-Wiring	55
Chapter	14	Tappity-Tap-Tap	58
Chapter	15	School Desk Factory	61
Chapter	16	Mountaintop Fish Pond	64
Chapter	17	Christmas Forgotten	68
Chapter	18	Raggedy Man	71
Chapter	19	School Lights	74
Chapter	20	Mountain Wild Flowers	77
Chapter	21	Turkey Rations	80
Chapter	22	The Church Bench	83
Chapter	23	Juan College	85
Chapter	24	Quiet Mountainside	90

Chapter 25	A Barrel of Honey	92
Chapter 26	Turkey Seed Stock	95
Chapter 27	Corn School	99
Chapter 28	The Painter's Party	103
Chapter 29	The Master Craftsman	106
Chapter 30	The Blanket Loom	111
Chapter 31	Little Rosa is Sick	115
Chapter 32	Jeep Coil-Checker	119
Chapter 33	Popcorn Sheeting	121
Chapter 34	Cement and Sherbet	127
Chapter 35	Toasted Peppers	130
Chapter 36	The Christmas Innkeeper	132
Chapter 37	Making Chicken Feed	136
Chapter 38	Witch Doctoring	139
Chapter 39	The Working Mothers	143
Chapter 40	Farm Wedding	148
Chapter 41	The Peanut Girl	152
Chapter 42	The Train Cars	155
Chapter 43	Bean Inoculation	159
Chapter 44	Loading the Bus	162
Chapter 45	The Sprinkling Can	165
Chapter 46	Angela's Joy	168
Chapter 47	Serendipity	171
Chapter 48	Camera Borrower	173
Chapter 49	My Backpack Book	175
Chapter 50	Village Square Chickens	177
Chapter 51	First Shoes	182

8

Chapter 52	The Family Trap	185
Chapter 53	Restaurant Ritual	188
Chapter 54	Nutrition Center	191
Chapter 55	Blind Vision	195
Chapter 56	Jeep Driving Lessons	198
Chapter 57	Garden Tutoring	202
Chapter 58	The Lost House	205
Chapter 59	The Hemophiliac	208
Chapter 60	Born on Holy Thursday	212
Chapter 61	Peace Corps Thanksgiving	215
Chapter 62	Moving Day	218
Chapter 63	Woman's Cannery	220
Chapter 64	A Tragic Gift	223
Chapter 65	Charcoal Market	226
Chapter 66	The Village Rooster	230
Chapter 67	The Lemon Harvest	234
Chapter 68	Family Moving Night	237
Chapter 69	Maria Isn't Here	240
Chapter 70	Pink School Desks	243
Chapter 71	Christmas Rejection	246
Chapter 72	Chicken Entrepreneur	248
Chapter 73	Mountain Jeep Ride	251
Chapter 74	A Grandmother's Legacy	253
Chapter 75	The Inspired Roofers	257
Chapter 76	The Photographer	259
Chapter 77	Man with Ten Cages	261
Chapter 78	God Will Repay You	264

This book is dedicated to all devoted human development volunteers. I give a special tribute to those with whom I have worked in the central highland villages of Guatemala, and the many hundreds who have followed, especially those who have come to serve at Common Hope in Guatemala.

Dave Huebsch

Foreword

My mother, who was a country schoolteacher, once told me the story of David and Goliath. She probably told me this story when I was a child because my name is David and she wanted to encourage me to be able to take a stand for the things in which I believed.

When she finished the story, she asked, "What was David thinking when he stepped out to do battle with Goliath, having only his sling and a few pebbles?"

"He must have been scared!" I remember saying as a small boy. "He was probably thinking that Goliath is so big and so strong, how could he ever win?"

"No," said my mother, "he was actually thinking something else. He was thinking that Goliath is so big, that how could he ever miss him?" My mother taught me to believe in myself and to handle large tasks without fear.

Leaving a comfortable teaching career and going off to the highland villages of Guatemala where we encountered vast numbers of children and families lost in poverty was like the story of Goliath. It was so large a task that we asked, "how could we ever make a difference?" The truth was, however, that we could hardly miss.

There are many of us who want to go where families are lost in the grip of poverty, and help them to rise from their unfortunate circumstances. Most people are unable to physically go and apply their time, skills, and resources because of their particular life situations and responsibilities. The evidence for this is the large number of people applauding and supporting those lucky few of us able to live out such an experience.

I have long been convinced that God could have chosen far better means than me to accomplish his purposes. There are so many others who are more gifted, insightful, and have greater resources than I, and who would certainly have been more effective in such work. I am forever grateful, however, that I was able to go and live out such an amazing encounter with the poorest of God's people.

This book is a series of episodes, which together present an insight into such a lifestyle. This mosaic of stories will demonstrate what such a life experience might have been like for anyone who might have gone as I have. It provides a means for the reader to vicariously experience such an adventure. Some of my experiences would certainly be very similar to those of someone else in the same circumstances.

This book is for ordinary people. People like myself who live normal ordinary lives, and do not think of their talents or abilities as extraordinary. This is also a book that encourages people to discover which of the elements of their lives are real and which are illusion. Those who have been volunteers will find themselves saying, "Yes, that is me also. I have been there, too. That has been my experience also!"

Many define themselves by what they've done and where they've been. Others are focused on what lies ahead and where their plans will lead them. What is most important, however, is not what lies behind us, or what lies before us, but what lies within us. This discovery is part of one's task in life.

We must remember that this is life; it's not a dress rehearsal. Each of us has been given an assignment, and there is much work to be done on them.

Dave Huelch

Chapter 1

An Original Child

It's a wonderful experience to encounter the children of the mountain villages. These are children who seldom leave their humble communities, and know little of the outside world. It's wonderful to know children who are totally unpretentious, and who are perfectly beautiful and unassuming.

There's a wonderful story about such an original child.

"How full is your pack, Abrams?" I asked, as we picked ripe oranges and loaded our backpacks on the sunny mountainside.

"I've only got room for these few more," said Abrams, as he stuffed them into his pack and zipped it shut. "Should we walk all the way down again, or should we head out cross country?" he asked.

"Do you know the way if we go cross country?" I asked. He responded by nodding and pointing the direction we must head. I checked my compass and said, "Let's go then."

We had been picking oranges and filling our backpacks from an orange grove we had planted years before. Then we set-off on our cross-country journey to visit a small village several hours distance by foot. We would be traveling across some pretty rugged terrain.

"We've been climbing this grade for more than an hour," I said. "Are you sure this is the best way?"

"There is loose volcanic gravel on the other side," he said. "We would be in the hot sun there, too. There's a cool stream of water when we get to the bottom of the next ravine."

I trusted Abrams. He was a Mayan Indian, born in these mountains. One day he taught me to know my position in that rough country by referencing the points of the three nearest volcanoes.

"I can see a tiny village across there," I said, pointing to a wisp of smoke rising from a tortilla fire probably. "We'll pass

through it in about half an hour don't you think?" I asked Abrams.

"Yes," he said, "it's on the way to the village where we're headed."

After several hours of travel, we came to that small village of about sixty houses, all of which were constructed of cane walls with dirt floors.

"Let's stop and rest under that mango tree there by those houses," said Abrams. "Getting across to this village was a good workout." So we took off our backpacks and sat down leaning back against a rickety bamboo building in the shade of that mango tree.

"The houses are all cane houses with dirt floors," I said. "And the people must grow corn up on the slopes of that volcano. I don't suppose they get many visitors," I added.

Soon curious children approached, innocent of the world of television, cartoons, and swing sets. They were the barefoot children of the cane houses and dirt floors. The bravest ones came near and smiling shook our hands first. "Hello," we were saying to them. "What is your name?" The others followed when we reached out and offered our hands to them, too.

When twenty or so of them were grouped around us, some sitting and still others standing and saying their names, there seemed to arise an awkward silence. I sensed the expectation of some entertainment, so I told them the "Big Mouth Frog" story.

It's a story where the frog speaks to other animals like the fox and tiger, and it's a simple children's story with animal animations and strange sounds. The children responded with unusual joy.

"Maybe my story is a hit," I thought, but then I remembered... "We've got the only show in town."

"These kids have never seen a person with light skin like yours," Abrams told me, indicating a couple of them who were putting their little brown arms beside mine to observe the difference.

"Let's give them each a half orange!" I suggested, getting out my Swiss army knife and unzipping my backpack.

"OK," said Abrams. "Then we won't have to carry these loads any further. Besides I don't think they have any oranges around here." I pealed my oranges as Abrams broke them in half and passed them to the children.

Next it was his turn to peal the oranges from his backpack, while I divided and handed half an orange to each of the remaining children. They were seedless, and ripe, and sweet. The children loved their first experience of perfectly ripened oranges.

"That's enough, they've all gotten one," I said. "How many do you have left?"

"None," said Abrams. "You're holding the last half orange."

Then we saw her, the bashful one, the round-eyed girl of about seven, shy and partly hidden behind a crumbling adobe wall. I offered her the last half orange that remained.

"Thanks," she said quietly, coming closer and reaching gently for the piece of orange. Then she did something I did not expect...

She took the half orange, broke it into two parts, and gave one part to her little brother beside her. Then she gave the other part to her little sister who was even more shy and hidden, peeking out from behind that crumbling wall. She thanked us and went off with not even a taste for herself. And we had nothing left to give her.

"I wasn't like that when I was a child, Abrams," I confessed. "I had a different way of sharing with my brothers and sisters!" We both just sat there silently watching her walk away with her brother on one side and her sister on the other side, each munching on savory pieces of an orange.

It was a year before I returned to that area. I found myself this time alone with a family where the father was gravely ill. "He has a very high fever," I said, putting my hand on his forehead. "How long has he been like this?" I asked his wife, whose face revealed her concern.

"It's been several days," she answered, "and the fever hasn't broken, and that's a bad sign." She touched his face with the back of her hand, moving her head negatively. He was burning up with an illness, probably pneumonia. He was lying on a mat of woven cornstalks, sometimes mumbling things that were completely unintelligible.

"Lord, we ask your blessing on this man. He is ill and we are asking that he become well again." I had a helpless feeling sitting on the dirt floor of their smoky cornstalk house, praying with this mother and her children, for this man who would probably die. I stayed with the mother and half dozen children and we talked and prayed until the darkness came.

We mostly talked, because after a while we ran out of prayer.

I hadn't noticed anything particular about the child sitting on the floor next to me, but I remember wanting to tell her that she needn't worry because things would get better, but I knew things would not get better.

"The truth was," I thought, "that things would probably get worse." I wanted to tell her brothers and sisters that they would go to school, and their father would live, and there would be plenty to eat...

"I have some food." I said, suddenly remembering some wheat buns I had in my backpack. "Here is a small bag of six or eight wheat buns," I said, taking the bag out of my backpack and handing it to the mother. I knew that often these families went with little or no food.

"Here, take this wheat bread," I said as I gave the last one, which I found loose in my backpack, to the child near me. To my surprise, she did an astonishing thing. .

She took the bread, said, "Thanks." Then she broke it, and gave half to her smaller brother and the other half to her little sister sitting beside me, and, although she had none left for herself, she seemed to expect nothing more.

"Now where had I seen that before?" I asked myself. Then I remembered the crumbling wall, and that last little girl receiving an orange.

That's how I recognized her… in the way she took the bread, said thanks, broke it, and gave it to her brother and sister. "Are you the little girl who got the last half orange…?" I began to ask. She was! She assented with a movement of her head.

"I recognized her in the breaking of the bread."

Later as I reflected on that, it was like hearing a voice asking, "Hey, haven't you learned to recognize me yet?" That's when I discovered the real attraction of working with the poor. I was also assured that I had been led to this place and this work, and that this was to be my assignment.

"Why am I so surprised to recognize His presence in so humble a child?" I thought, "I shouldn't be surprised at all, because that's exactly where He Himself said that we could expect to find Him."

Chapter 2

Life is too Fragile

"We lack proper medical facilities here in this very large village," said a doctor who worked with us in a very sizable village on the highland lake. "When there is an emergency there is no place to turn."

What do you do when emergencies can't be handled in your office," I asked.

"They need to be transported to a hospital two hours away around the mountains," he said, "and that is too long a wait, and too far on rough mountain roads. Especially with a population like we have here, of forty thousand people."

One morning there was just such a family emergency!

"Danny is sick!" they were saying. "The doctor says we have to get him to the hospital!"

It seems that their six-year-old son had become sick. One of the local doctors had diagnosed him as having appendicitis. The road to the nearest hospital is a twisting mountain road with switchback turns and steep winding climbs. The word 'incredible' comes to mind.

"I'll drive you in the van," I offered. "We will take him to the hospital on the other side of the lake." We could see the hospital clearly from where we stood. It was just across the lake. It takes us two hours on horrible narrow mountain roads to get there in the van.

The child's father rushed him into the van and into Betty's waiting arms, flying blanket and all!

His parents came along to keep him comfortable, and the Dodge van we drove gave quite a comfortable ride in spite of the condition of the road. His condition was indeed critical.

"I'll come along to sit up front," said Jeff, the child's teacher. "I'll help watch the road."

Most of the road was a twisting mountain dirt road with

chuckholes and rocks sticking up here and there. Most people wouldn't want to even watch, as we sailed around the hairpin turns where there were sheer drops.

The child was in quite a bit of discomfort. Betty was doing what she could to keep him comfortable and reassure the concern of his parents.

"You're not afraid of these roads," commented Jeff.

"Not really," I said. "Oh, something could go wrong, or we could make a bad move on a narrow hairpin curve and go flying off the edge I suppose. We figure that it was so far down to the canyon below that if we did go off the road, we'd have time for a full confession before we hit bottom," I said laughing.

"The child is not good," said Jeff.

After the first hour of this, things began to go bad for the child. I saw the concern on the father's face in my mirror, and I sensed the growing tension in the mother's voice as she tried to speak gently to the boy.

We didn't make it.

Life is too fragile. All we could do was not enough. We were only ten minutes from the hospital when we lost him. I asked them at the hospital to do an autopsy so we could know the cause of death.

"He had died of typhoid," said the doctor.

"It's the unsanitary living conditions in their village," I thought. "The rainy season leaves puddles of water which turn stagnant in the streets and green in the heat of the morning sun."

"There was nothing more that you could do," I said to the father, who was trying to conceal the pain written all over his face. "It doesn't surprise me that it was typhoid fever and not appendicitis." Most villagers carried their drinking water from the lake where they also bathed and washed their clothes. Quite a number of people in this village had died of typhoid recently, so we were not surprised. No effort on our part would have saved him.

We were sad to have an empty desk in one of our schools.

We are very ordinary people and to be honest it sometimes takes all the faith we have, to stay with it. We knew the pain of losing a child having lost two of our own when they were children.

It seemed strange to be so well prepared to work with people in these particular difficulties. In this village, they buried two children every day on the average, and we never ran out of compassion or became complacent about it.

"It hurts to lose a child," we told them, instinctively knowing what they needed. "We'll stay with you until there is more family here to help you through the rest of the day." In this village we had no monopoly on children who have died. Almost every family had lost children here.

"There was nothing we could do," said the father, repeating my words when it came time for us to leave.

Two weeks later the same family lost another little boy. Again we were able to stay and help them through it.

We also know that wherever life takes you, the road's going to have some bumps and turns. We've spent too many years teaching in a Minnesota High School and raising our own family, to think that we have any kind of inside track about difficult roads.

A few days later some of the village nurses caught up with me and said, "You're going to have to take a dose of your own medicine now."

"Why me?" I asked, looking at the needle. "I've had my shot! I got my shot yesterday," I lied.

"Because you're so stupid!" they said, "you're so reckless, and you expose yourself to typhoid all the time... So roll up your sleeve!" I would have gotten away, except that there was a group of children there watching, and I didn't want to be a bad example for them.

We had brought enough typhoid vaccine into the village to inoculate the population. The nurses who were doing that work for us were a little too thorough to suit me.

True, we may have an empty school desk... But there are thousands of school desks that are filled with a generation of children getting their first chance at a better life. These children get hot lunches every day, and they're learning to read and write, and they're learning more about health care every day.

They are getting soap and toothbrushes, food and school supplies. We hear them reciting their lessons. Sometimes we hear them singing.

One day I heard the children singing from a classroom down the street. It was the sound of alleluias gently filling the air.

Chapter 3

Street Magic

Do you believe in magic? The village children always beg me to do magic tricks. I love to see their amazed faces, and I think that's what encourages me. I think some of them really believe I can do magic!

"See this penny?" I say, holding up a penny for all of the children to see. Then I put the penny in the palm of my other hand... slowly then, I open first one hand then the other. "Where is the penny?" I ask.

They never cease to be amazed! "Where is it? Where is it?" they ask.

"There it is," I answer. "It's there in your ear!" Then I reach my hand towards their ear producing the missing coin.

I can do the exact same trick an endless number of times, and they will all still want to see it once more. They think I can make pennies disappear and then reappear again from under rocks, under their chins, and from their pockets.

"I'm going to throw this penny up into the air," I tell them. And I make a throwing motion as though throwing the penny upwards. "See it?" I ask as I move my pointing finger, following it's imaginary flight looping around through the air. Suddenly, "Clap!" I go with my hand and point to a rock lying innocently on a nearby wall.

"Go look!" I say still pointing to the rock.

"It's here!" the first one to see it will shout. And they will run back to me with the penny saying, "do it again," handing me the penny.

My uncle Henry did a little magic when I was a child. My aunt Kate had a player piano and a little cabinet with a glass door where she kept dozens of piano rolls.

"See this key," I remember Uncle Henry saying, taking the key from the little cabinet.

All of us children would sit on the floor in a circle around him, watching his every movement.

"I'm taking the little key," he would say, showing it to each of us, "and I'm putting the key on my tongue," and we would then watch as he placed the little key carefully on his tongue.

He would then go through some swallowing motions, pretending to swallow the little key. We children were totally convinced that he had swallowed the key for sure.

"That was good," he would say, patting his stomach.

Uncle Henry's trick was to first show us his empty hand, then reach slowly to his ear, and seem to pull the little cabinet key magically out of his ear.

"Here it is again," he would say, as we children would sit there and look at that key in utter amazement.

Well I believed it! Later, after he left, I tried it out. I took the key, laid it on my tongue, and swallowed it… but it wouldn't come out of my ear.

All of my little cousins quickly tattled to Kate. "Dave swallowed the little key!" they said, and there was no hushing them.

"Dave, what have you done? Did you swallow my little cabinet key?" asked my aunt Kate.

"Dave, why did you do that?" asked my mother.

I don't think my aunt Kate ever forgave me. Twenty years later the piano rolls were still all locked up in that cabinet. She denied herself the pleasure of ever listening to another piano roll as long as she lived. She wouldn't hear of opening that cabinet some other way.

Anyway, the village children liked magic tricks and so I put on my little street show for them sometimes. I was always careful not to pretend to swallow anything as part of the trick. I mostly used pennies, rocks, and sticks for the tricks. Once I stashed a bunch of pennies under many rocks and in the crevices of the adobe walls of my outdoor street-theater before the children arrived.

One old woman watched for awhile, believed it was really magic, and accused me of using the power of the devil to make those coins disappear and appear everywhere...

"You are using the power of the devil!" she said, pointing an accusing finger at me.

"No, no," I said. "It's not the power of the devil at all." Then I showed her in slow-motion how the coin really didn't disappear at all. From then on, she watched the tricks with that sort of grin on her face as if to say, "How can those children believe that this is really magic?"

Once when a little audience had gathered for my street tricks, we stopped for a moment and I began telling them about the new school we were planning for them.

"Where will the new school be?" some of them asked.

Then I showed them the place on the mountainside of jagged rocks that would soon become their beautiful new school.

"It will be right here," I said as I walked over and showed them, motioning with my arms, where the school would be.

"OK, Do it!" said one of the children as they all turned and waited expectantly for the new school to suddenly appear ...just like my other tricks.

I was embarrassed by their faith in me.

The school was eventually built by community volunteers. The men each worked two or three days each month. The women worked in groups making the noon lunches. We supplied some tools, buckets, steel, and cement. They cut the timbers in the mountains and then sawed them up into lumber, dug out for the foundations, tied the steel, mixed cement with hoes, laid blocks and stones, and tiled the roof. On days when we poured foundations or floors, hundreds of workers showed up to help.

This community never had a school before. Instead of us building it for them, they built it for themselves. They were so very proud of their school.

All I did was give them permission to do it. At the dedication of the school, to symbolize ownership by the community I presented the President of the Education Committee with a ceremonial key, remembering the key that I had swallowed so many years before.

The new school eventually did appear... almost magically!

Chapter 4

The Boy and the Soldiers

There was a neighborhood boy named Eric of about twelve or thirteen who liked to help me especially when it involved taking mechanical things apart to fix them. "Here you are," I'd say when he seemed to appear out of nowhere as if by magic, "and just in time to help me wire up this compressor."

"Why do you connect that white wire to that green one," he would ask.

"Because we don't have a good ground," I answered.

"Why don't we have a good ground?" was the next question.

"Because here on the volcano with all of the volcanic ash and volcanic rock, they don't often install or need a good ground, because it's like walking on an insulator," I tried to explain.

"What's the difference between volcanic rock and other soil?"

"When you're standing on regular soil, you can get a big shock of electricity," I began. "But if you're on volcanic rock, you're more like a bird sitting on the wires outside."

"Why don't the birds on the wires get shocks of electricity?" he asked next... And so that's how his lessons on electricity progressed, and how my lesson on patience advanced at the same time.

He wanted to learn about electricity and wiring and why things worked the way they did. He was full of questions.

We were remodeling the building we were in. We were converting it into a family center to serve poor families in the area. It was once a place where volunteers lived; next it was used by the military as a stopover place. When we took it over we had to haul out all of the sand bags they used for bunkers, replace all of the wiring and plumbing, and patch up thousands of bullet holes everywhere.

Every once in awhile groups of soldiers would come back

and expect to stay there because they didn't know it was no longer available to them. We never wanted to challenge the soldiers or try to argue with them.

It's like they guy who had a pet tiger, and a reporter asked him once where the tiger sleeps. "Wherever he wants to sleep," came the answer. This situation was like that for the first few months.

"Get that wire cutter," I said to Eric, as I watched him get the tool in his hand, "Now cut that black wire even with the white one," I instructed. He loved to cut the wires and strip them. "Do you know the gauge of the wire? And can you strip it back about a half-inch?"

"Yes," he answered and stripped both of the wires.

It was beginning to grow a little dark, and it was time to quit pretty soon. "What is this thing anyway?" Eric asked.

"It's an old milk cooler from a school," I answered. "It was used to dispense milk, and we are making it into a little refrigerator."

"There are some soldiers outside," said Eric.

"That's OK," I answered without looking up. "We were here first."

"No," he said, "I'm serious… There are a lot of them."

"Then we'll just get ready and fight them off!" I joked. "Go look out the window and see how many there are so we know how many bullets we will need… See if it's a whole company that we are up against."

When he came back he said, "I think it's a whole division!" I noticed that his voice was kind of shaky. When I finally looked at him, he was as white as paper. He was completely scared and holding onto my shoulder by now.

I could clearly see that something was very wrong. I would have to get him out of here now, and back to his house.

"Eric," I said, "you know how we have often talked about your uncle who has that little store down the street. He thinks that he is the great champion soccer player, and likes to give a play-by-play of every game he's in."

"Yeah," he said, still a little frightened.

"Well," I said, "we're going to leave now. We're going to

walk right out of that door and walk right through the middle of those soldiers like they're not even there. As we do that, we are going to keep talking about your uncle and his silly play-by-plays. We are just going to walk casually. I will be with you every step of the way."

I took my little toolbox in hand, and out we headed together talking about his uncle and his soccer episodes. And never once did either of us look at the soldiers or even acknowledge that they were there.

There was at least a division of soldiers.

I learned later that one year before, another group of soldiers came to his house and took his father away with them by force, and he was still missing.

Chapter 5

The Widow's Chickens

"The more you do, the more we help you do, and the less you do, the less we help you do," I explained to one of the widows. I was explaining to her about how we like to work with families. That was our general working policy with the poor families with which we worked.

"It's the opposite of welfare," we often said. However, there were too many families to work with them all at once. We had to get some of them independent and on their own, so they could become part of our team in helping to teach their neighbors.

"Can we raise chickens, too?" they would ask about our most popular food project.

"If everyone who asked would actually raise chickens, we'd have a thousand cages in every village," I explained to several women wanting to begin. I had designed the chicken-raising project so it could be done successfully by people who neither read nor write, and the work could be completed in only about thirty minutes each day by a ten-year-old.

That's why it was popular. Each month they would have more protein in their diet, and a few chickens to sell for a good price. "This is a very profitable business," said one of the women, "and little Rosita can take care of it by herself."

"You have to follow my instructions about this investment," I would always say to the new ones, "until you have made money on five successful cages of chickens."

I think that was the hard part for them. They didn't understand the word "investment." They didn't know anything about protein, fat, and fiber either. They didn't understand about profit and margin. "I will have to teach them," I thought to myself.

So we began with those in greatest need. We began with the widows, especially those who were illiterate, beginning with those who had many children. We easily found a dozen of them. My teaching method might not have been orthodox, but it seemed to work well... most of the time.

"You get a cage to use," I instructed Marta, "along with the little feeder, the water jar, the sack of corn and grinder, and the pre-mixed concentrate." Then I would give them the sixteen baby chickens, and the little light-bulb heater that kept the chicks warm for the first week or ten days.

I often set the box of baby chicks a little distance away from the cage. "Make a line here," I'd say to them, "from this box here to the cage door." Then I would line up all the children and mother between the box of chicks and the door of the cage. The truth was that they were all dying to touch those little yellow baby chicks, and by passing the chicks one to another on their way to the cage, they seemed to get touching the chicks out of their system.

The first day all the children wanted to grind the corn. They all wanted to prepare the gallon water jar and flip it over so the birds could drink.

"Put a couple of your marbles in the bottom of the drinker," I'd say to the children. And they'd run a get a couple of marbles.

"Why did we put those marbles there?" they'd ask.

"See how the little chicks are curious and try to peck at those shiny marbles?" I'd ask. "When they peck at the shiny marbles, they get a mouthful of water, right?" I continued, "so that's how you are

now the teachers, teaching them where the water is and how to drink."

Then I'd make surprise visits over the next seven weeks while the chicks were growing. I'd check for feed, water, and general care. They knew that they could lose their cage if things were not well in hand. They had all of the supplies up front, so there were no excuses.

At the end of the eighth week it was time to market the chickens. That was the most fun of all! I'd come prepared. I'd have the supplies with me for the next flock, but I'd keep the feed and new little chicks hidden in the back of my jeep.

I would always bring along some chicken buyers who would buy the full grown chickens, and later resell them in the large open markets. When we arrived at Marta's cage, I hung up my scale and weighed each chicken, wrote down the pounds and ounces, and then put each chicken into the buyer's slatted box. When all the chickens were weighed, we would add up the amounts, and the buyer would give me the cash money according to the agreed upon price.

Then came the fun! I told Marta how much money the feed had cost, and counted out that much money and put it into an envelope marked "feed" before unloading the new sacks of feed for the new flock. Then I told her how much the chicks cost, and put that much money into another envelope, before getting out the new box of chicks.

Then I counted out the rest of the money and gently laid it in Marta's hand. She looked at it for a long time because it was a lot of money... more than she had seen in one place for a long time.

"And this?" she questioned, "what is this for?" She still didn't understand. These were her profits. This is money she had earned!

"This is for your work in taking good care of the chickens," I explained. "This is your money because you have earned it!" I further explained that she had also paid for her next cage of chickens and for all of the feed they would eat before going to market.

She began speaking now with tears in her eyes. "Tomorrow we will go to the market and buy shoes for Rosita for school. There will be spools of thread for weaving, too, but we will save most of the money for times when we will need it."

A neighbor woman who was her good friend was there, too. She helped with catching the chickens and weighing them. She saw her friend's success with the chicken cage.

"Can I get a cage of chickens to raise, too?" she asked.

"Well," I began, "this cage project is only for widows so far because we have only enough funds for three hundred cages. I don't know you very well," I continued cautiously. "Are you a widow?"

She thought about what I had said and responded in the strangest way with only the word "almost." I was never sure just what that meant, but I hope she wasn't thinking about knocking her husband over the head just to get a chicken cage. I figured it was best not to question her meaning further.

Chapter 6

Orphanage Repairs

There was an orphanage on the other side of the village run by a nun from the local parish. I must say that I do not believe in orphanages because there are better ways of caring for abandoned children.

"Place the children with extended family," I would argue. "Then we can help that whole family more, so they can rise faster from their conditions." That was my thinking on the matter. "We're in the development business, not the band-aid business."

Every now and then some North American would adopt a child and take them back to the States. "They are better off," would be the claim, "and they'll give them a better life."

"So... Now we're exporting people?" I'd ask.

And so the argument continued. They had a point, too. "Besides an orphanage makes a good fundraiser!" I'd say in an attempt to get in the last word. The nun who ran the place was a very good friend of mine, and I know that if we didn't argue about that, we'd quickly find something else to argue about anyway.

She hated anything military! I wasn't crazy about military things either, but I soon learned the fun of pushing that button of hers from time to time...

"Did you put that little toy soldier on my desk?" she would demand.

"I? Would I do something like that? Maybe one of your smart-alecky orphans did that," I'd suggest. I probably blamed the orphans for things pretty often. She didn't know that I had bought a large bag of two-inch rubber toy soldiers with jeeps, trucks, guns, and tanks. I bought them as a gift for her, and would be giving them to her one at a time over the next year.

"The washing machine's broken," said one of the orphans standing in our doorway one day, panting from running so far.

"Have you taken it apart yet?" I asked not expecting an answer.

"If you come right away, you can give me a ride back to the orphanage in your jeep," said the street-wise eight-year-old.

"Now that sounded like something I might have said," I thought to myself. "I'll get my tools." I hated to fix the washer all the time. Something would be broken and then we'd have to find the parts, and that was always a pain. Then by the time I was able to put the machine back together, I'd forgotten how I had taken it apart."

"Sometimes I have to look for my washer parts where the children have been playing. Why don't you get them some real toys?" I'd complain.

So… If I gave her an occasional toy soldier, it was completely justified.

This time the washing machine had a real problem. The main bearing was shot. "The weight of everything sits on this bearing," I thought. "And where will I ever find another one to replace it? It's no wonder it's shot, the way they stuff this machine with clothes when they use it!"

It's like the joke about how many people fit on a bus. The answer is, "ten more!" How many clothes can you stuff in the washer? The answer is, "it depends on whether you tamp them in with a two-by-four so you can get the cover down!"

I brought the ruined roller bearing down to the project house

with me, because I'd have to find another one to replace it. Later I got to thinking that maybe I could make one. "I'll try to make one out of plastic," I thought.

"Get me a bunch of old clean plastic bags," I said to the orphan who was still with me. I think the Sister assigned him to watch me.

"How many is a 'bunch,'" he asked.

"Get two bunches," I answered, and off he ran.

I put the plastic bags in a frying pan and turned on the heat a little in an attempt to melt them. When they started to melt together and look like a weird omelet, I turned off the heat, and used the spatula I was ruining to gather the plastic together on a heap in the middle of the pan. I kept shaping it as it cooled to look like a thick miniature hockey puck.

It became really hard and felt slippery to my fingers. This was good. When it was cold, I drilled out the center hole the same size as the old bearing, and ground down the edge so it would have the correct outside diameter.

"It's a 'slip' bearing," I said to the orphan, who now was a different orphan. I think they were taking turns watching me. "This is better than a roller bearing," I continued, "because we don't have a roller bearing."

…And it worked. I was quite amazed because it actually worked for many years.

Then, before leaving, I left one of my little two-inch rubber "military calling cards" on sister's desk, pointing his little gun at her copy of *Peace and Justice* leaning against her stack of books.

Chapter 7

Women vs. Builders

Unless I could judge favorably for both sides, I wouldn't ever want to be a judge. I think I'd rather be in the middle of the trouble!

Once we were doing a little building project, which stirred up a little problem that needed a decision. We were building a small six-classroom school on some very marginal land. It was actually positioned near the side of the mountain just as most of the buildings in this village were.

The village people had a tradition of arguing forever over every two inches of land. A surveyor would cost them more money than they hoped to make in a lifetime, so they never went to court... they just argued. The lots were small; a large one would be perhaps six meters by eight meters.

The corners of lots were marked with a particular variety of small tree, which simply invited argument.

There was no such thing as a street or border that was straight. The streets and paths not only curved back and forth and around, but up and down as well. If a person didn't know the village, it was very easy to get lost.

One can easily pass the same spot two or three times before getting to one's destination.

One day I went to that school construction location to see how things were going. It wasn't good. A huge argument had arisen about the pathway winding down around the backside of the school. The pathway was necessary for the hundreds of houses above the school.

It seems that the men had laid the first row of stones for the back wall of the school. The problem was that they had laid them on the very edge of the descending pathway.

"There's plenty of space to pass by on that pathway," I heard one of the builders say.

"No," said one of the women in the gathering crowd of women who came, attracted by the rising of voices. "There won't be enough space!"

The men huddled together to talk among themselves for a minute. "Well, the land is part of the land deeded for the school," said the spokesman.

"Do you want us to measure it again?" asked another of the men.

Then one woman explained in more detail that if the wall were to rise where it was, there might be room for a person to walk on the pathway between the mountainside and the wall…

"That's what we've been telling you," said the spokesman interrupting her and nodding his head. "There's lots of room to walk there."

"But," continued the woman loudly, "we can no longer put our baskets on our heads and carry them up and down the pathway! Our baskets are too wide and won't fit through that space." It seems that she was right. Women had been carrying baskets up and down this passageway for more than a thousand years maybe, and they must have a right of passage to carry baskets from the

market down below.

The men claimed legal rights to the land. The women claimed an ancient right to their passage. The men were looking at the row of blocks already laid, and at the width of the path on the ground where their feet were. The women were thinking about the width of the path up where their baskets needed lots of free space for movement and balancing.

That's when they became aware that I was standing within hearing distance. It's partly my fault that I got involved because I should have had enough sense to get away from there. Then they came to me and wanted me to be the judge and decide for them!

So I took a look at the building plans, got out my tape measure and checked the measurements. I soon ran out of delay tactics. Then I suddenly realized that some of these women were wives of some of the men... so I got an idea.

"If you women can no longer carry your corn up this path, you can no longer make tortillas for your families can you?" I asked.

"No we can't," they said together nodding their heads and folding their arms in unison. "and we can't carry the clothes down to the lake to wash them either, so our families just have to wear dirty clothes."

Then I gathered the men back into their huddle and asked them what they wanted to do. "We want to move the wall," they all agreed quietly.

So... then I announced my judgment against the men and to have the wall moved. At which they all smiled and shook my hand and got right back to work. I may have saved them from months of arguments and perhaps several broken marriages, who knows?

But it was pretty clear that I'm a better politician, than I am a judge!

Chapter 8

White Door-Cross

Many people were being hurt by Guatemala's civil war violence. In one village where we worked extensively, there were five hundred widows as a result of the violence.

"It's really hard for me," one widow named Josefa, said to me. "We were poor before my husband was killed, but now I'm not only poor, I'm alone, and with these four children to raise." There remained a great deal of unresolved anger, and her children had witnessed horrible events.

Both widows and children were victims of the violence.

"My house is very small and humble. We have to cook inside and there is always a bit of smoke in the house," Josefa said to me the first time I went to see her. "Oh," she said, when I entered her little house, "don't worry about the door. The hinges are broken and it won't close all the way."

"You have a very nice little house," I said, "It seems very comfortable here." She had flowers and plants growing out of broken jars and some larger potted plants were outside.

We worked with most of these widows so they could raise more food and perhaps sell something at the open market to make some money. "How are the chickens growing," I asked. "How long before they will go to market?"

"We're going to run short of chicken feed, I think," she said looking away from me. "They're eating so much these days!" She was lying. She told me that because they had run out of food themselves, and they borrowed some of the chicken's corn and made tortillas out of it to eat.

"Yes," I agreed. "They eat a lot more when they get nearer to market time." I would never expose her little lie. How can she feed her chickens all the corn they want, when her children are hungry?

"Have you thought about getting a second cage of chickens?"

"I can't afford to get another cage," she said quietly. "Don't we have to pay for the second cage?"

"Yes," I answered. "That's the rule for the wire chicken cages; however, I have an idea of how you could get another cage or even two." Her eyes brightened so I continued, "You still have space for two more cages here in your yard. Well, I have a bamboo cage that's not being used. I will set that cage up here," I said indicating where the cage would be placed.

"Wouldn't I have to pay for it?" she asked.

"I'll make a deal with you," I said. "I'll set it here for you to use. If Antonio can copy it, and make another one just like it out of bamboo, you can have both bamboo cages."

"Antonio can build a new cage, but we don't have any bamboo because it doesn't grow up this high on the mountain."

"I'll bring it the next time I come by," I said. "We always have lots of bamboo. Antonio's new cage will have to pass my inspection, though."

"By the way," I told her, "I bought ten pounds of corn at the market earlier for our own chickens, but I made a mistake and got the kind of corn that's used for tortillas, not chicken feed."

"I don't know what to do with it." I said. "Would you be willing to take this corn off our hands?" It was my turn now to tell a lie.

It took a few weeks, but her eleven-year-old, Antonio, finally finished the bamboo cage. It was worth waiting for, just to see the pride in Josefa's eyes.

"Josefa," I said to her, "I noticed that many of you widows have a large two foot cross roughly painted on your wooden house doors in white paint."

She explained how their priest, whose life had also been taken by the violence two years before, painted it there to remind them that, in spite of all that has happened, they are Christians.

She said, "it means that Jesus was a victim, too, and that we would have to be forgiving just as he was." She explained how seeing that cross many times each day helped her to identify with being forgiving.

I don't often get by with asking about something like that. The women have a way of turning the tables on every conversation...

"Now it's your turn," Josefa said to me. "Explain the little cross that's dangling from your neck." I was wearing my little TEC cross that I got from the Central Minnesota TEC retreat program. So, I took it off and handed it to her so she could see it close up. Then I explained that this cross that I wore, had only an outline of the image of Jesus on it.

"My cross is a reminder, too, like yours," I further explained. "Whenever I see the outline image on the cross, it reminds me that it's up to me to become the image."

Later that week I brought some garden seed to their house and checked their food project. The nine-year-old girl who was home told me how her mother had gathered the family that evening.

"Mom explained to us about the cross you wear," she said, pointing to the cross hanging around my neck. "She told us what the image meant."

"I've been wearing this cross for more than ten years," I told her, handing her the cross to see the outline image.

"Mom told us that from now on, the big white cross on our door, which has no image, means that we all had to become the images of Jesus, too."

Chapter 9

Chiseled School

I met with many of the parents of one mountain village who are dreaming of having a real school for their children. We've been renting some space, but it's very crowded for the hundreds of children who come. One of the classrooms had eighty-five children without desks, chalkboards, or even lights.

"Having a good school for our children is our dream," said a very nervous woman with the courage to speak up at the large meeting. She was expressing the opinion of most of the people of that community.

I usually have two choices in these matters. I can struggle against it for a long time, and then do it... or I can just do it. I always come out second best in these dealings.

"We have estimated that the cash outlay to complete the school," I told them, "will be eighty thousand dollars. We have only fifteen hundred dollars in the account for this building project so far."

"What can we do to help?" asked one man sitting with a small group. These people had lots of determination. They seemed to understand that the only thing more expensive than education is the lack of it.

"Are you people willing to begin?" I asked the crowd, already knowing the answer. "We can begin," I continued, "but we may have to stop and wait for more money a couple of times?" One could sense a general rise in the level of the excitement of the huge group gathered in the large open space where the school was to be built.

So it was decided... We were going to begin! "It seemed a little like inviting everyone over for dinner," we decided, "but not knowing if there will be enough bread for them all." But, we also knew that God never calls us to the task, without providing us with all of the resources.

We planned another community meeting of the two or three thousand families, on a large open space on the mountainside. Most everybody came and they all agreed about a school. The project would pay for an architect, and supply the tools and the materials that would have to be purchased, but they would build it and it would be their school.

We would meet again in one week. In the meantime I got a rugged volcanic rock from the mountain, got a chisel and hammer, and sat in the main square of the village, and began chipping away at this hunk of rock. I had no idea if I could actually make a stone building block out of this or not.

"What are you making?" the people passing by would stop and ask.

"We are building a school here in this community," I'd answer simply. "This is the first building block of thousands that will be needed." Of course they knew that we were building a school. You had to be from another planet not to know that.

"What are you making out of that particular rock?" they would ask. Some of them laughed because it would take the rest of my life to chip out enough blocks to build a school. They didn't quite have the vision yet for this very bold community project.

I barely got it done in time for the community meeting.

"Each family would chip out one stone block each week." I

suggested to the even larger crowd that gathered. Then I said to them, "If a Gringo like myself can do it, all of you certainly could do it."

There were shouts of agreement! This stone chipping was widely accepted by a show of hands. My days of chipping and being laughed at were now paying off. I think it may have actually inspired the people to begin chipping their own stone blocks.

"Each family also needs to supply one volunteer worker for three days each month," I announced. The crowd quickly accepted this idea as well.

It was important for us to have them do their part... that's was part of our vision for giving ownership and dignity to the poor with whom we work. The good news is that the families immediately began chipping the large volcanic rocks into building blocks, using my block as a pattern.

"We are going to build a school on our mountainside!" they would say when I asked what they were making. "It will take time," one of them said, "but with simple hammers and chisels we will chip a school out of that mountainside."

"We've been having thirty workers here every day," the building director told me, "and we haven't run short of hand-chipped stone blocks." The entire cost of the school was greatly reduced. Even the mothers helped. This is the largest and poorest section of the poorest village we have yet seen.

Finally, the people appointed a day to dedicate their new school.

"We are very proud of what we have done!" the people were saying. It was the talk of the marketplace. Their pride and joy was obvious...

"The men went out early this morning fishing," the women said as we unloaded sacks of sugar and corn and flour from our van. "We will bake bread and make tortillas now, and when the men return with their catch, we will fry their fish," the women said.

Even the children ran into the mountains gathering herbs from which a salad was made.

When all was prepared, the president of their new school board got up and proudly led us in a short prayer and some words of dedication. He mentioned that this was the first time anyone could recall, that they had ever done anything together as a community… and we sat and broke bread together and you could sense their pride in what they had done.

Then something strange happened… A sudden hush fell… Even the children stopped suddenly in their play… The men were eating silently and invariably turning their faces toward this work they had built… The people grew strangely quiet… Each family could probably see the particular stone blocks they had chipped. Even I looked at the stone that I had chipped which had now become the cornerstone.

"We chiseled that school out of the mountainside," everyone was thinking.

But now they were seeing their individual stones combined into something larger than any one of them. The women looked at their husbands with pride… The men looked at this school that had risen out of the earth. They ate, and they wiped their cheeks. One could sense that something very great was taking place…

"This is the moment in their history," I thought to myself, "when they are becoming a people." This community experience suggests to me the difficulty of God's will being done on earth, without our willingness to step forward to begin the task of our assignment.

Someone said to me not long ago, "You're a person of great faith!" Well, I'm not so sure that it's faith! For me it's more of a queasy feeling in my stomach, whenever I begin on what appears to be a foolish journey, without map or compass.

…I only wish my stomach believed that it's faith.

Chapter 10

A Shattered Roof

"Almost time to go to the airport…" My father and my son, John, were flying to Guatemala today for a week. They were coming to see us and learn more about what we were doing.

"I have to check with the men working on the roof before we go," I answered. I wanted to see if they needed anything before we left. So I headed up the ladder and began crossing the roof to where several men were making repairs.

I was just beginning to speak to them as I crossed the roof, when I suddenly felt the sheet of fiberlite roofing on which I was walking begin to break-up under my feet.

"Ahaieeee!" came out of my mouth, as I felt myself falling through the roof, the dozens of pieces of broken roofing falling with me. I sucked in my breath as I fell and in doing so I also sucked in all of the loose chaff and seeds fallen from the avocado tree which had gathered in loose piles on the roof which had broken up.

The avocado chaff filled my mouth and throat and practically choked me.

And I just fell with the pieces of roof, and I remember landing fourteen feet below on the cement floor directly on my butt. And I remember bouncing like the pieces of broken up tiles that fell with me.

There was lots of pain, but my first problem was breathing because my throat and mouth were full of that loose chaff. I tried to blow it out of my mouth, but I had to first get some air into my lungs. I couldn't do that so I just started to spit and use my fingers to clear my mouth.

It seemed like forever before I could get some air …

By that time the workers had gotten down the ladder and were around me and trying to stand me up, and trying to make me walk.

"If he can walk, he will be alright" they must have been thinking.

"But I shouldn't be upright and trying to walk," I was thinking, "I may have broken bones." I was beginning to become aware of the pain by now, which seemed to come shooting from everywhere. Then I got a second and a third breath and was able to get much of the dry chaff out of my mouth.

"I will live," I lied. Then I forced a little grin. I just wanted them to let me lie somewhere and not try to make me walk. Then they laid me down again.

"Get around on that other side," said the one who seemed to take charge. "OK, all together, now," and I felt myself gently lifted by many, many small brown hands and carried what seemed about half a block.

Then they laid me back down on what seemed to be a wood surface. I was puzzled about where I was. "What is this wood surface?" I thought.

"OK men, slowly now," I heard one say. Then I became aware of the wood surface slowly beginning to move.

It was the old high-wheeled ox-cart! They didn't have time to hitch up the oxen, so they all took hold somewhere, some pulling on the front poles, pushing on the high wheels, or on the back.

The streets were passable with a four-wheel drive if you choose your path carefully. There were rocks, some partly buried in the street, everywhere.

I lay on the cart like a slab of beef, powerless to move myself now, and tossed back and forth, subject to every jerk and pitch of the cart as it traveled over the rocks. I made short low-pitched groans every time the cart pitched.

People came out of their little houses and cornstalk huts to see us pass by. Children came running. In between my own little shouts, I heard people shouting to each other.

The men pushing and pulling the cart were trying to go over the rocks as gently and quickly as possible. I must have been a real spectacle lying there, pitching back and forth like a slab of beef going through the center of this village.

And that's they way we traveled the twelve blocks through that entire village to the clinic on the other side, where they were taking me to see the Indian doctor.

He tried to examine me right there on the cart. He rolled me back and forth for his examination. By now hundreds of people were around the cart helping him examine me. I saw faces everywhere filled with concern, some wiping their eyes, others trying to talk to me.

Then he gave me a shot and they loaded me into an old panel truck that had been repainted to look like an ambulance. Off we went then to the city hospital four hours away.

I had come to these people to help them in their poverty, and here they were, helping me instead, at a time of my great need.

Chapter 11

The Turtle Shell

"Watch where they put my shoes and clothes," I said. "I have no intention of staying in this hospital. I feel pretty good already!"

I was almost embarrassed that I had made a spectacle of myself earlier in the village. "We've got to get to the airport because the plane will be landing soon," I said. I wondered why they had me in a hospital gown just to take an x-ray.

By now I was walking around and feeling much better. The doctor came with a gurney and rolled me away to get an x-ray. Then they rolled me back again... and we waited.

"Your back is broken," was their news. "It's the seventh vertebra."

"Why don't I feel any pain then?" I asked, thinking that they've made a mistake.

"Because we gave you shots that took away all of your pain," the doctors said. And at that, they rolled me into a room, slid me into a bed and that's where I stayed for the next ten dismal days.

They kept pricking me with things by my legs and feet. They said that I had a "crushed" vertebra, and there is a very high chance that I would never walk again. They took lots of x-rays. I didn't know what they were going to do to try to fix me.

It hurt when I laughed. I couldn't have the bed rolled up because it hurt when I bent upwards. So I lay flat most of the time. Eating was a difficulty.

I had to slide the food off of my plate into my mouth. It was kind of messy. "At least I didn't have a whole village watching," I thought to myself.

"So... how are you feeling?" asked my Dad when he came to visit me there before he and the others went out to the village the next day.

"OK, I guess. I'm doing the best I can," I answered. "I don't know how many days I'll be here, but someone will show you around."

"I must look pretty dreadful." I thought, "because my dad stood there not saying much… just looking at me while the others carried the conversation more." I saw a tear streak down first one cheek and then the other, but that was the only clue about his feelings. I knew that he was getting uncomfortable.

It's the only time in my life that I have ever seen my father weep.

I was sorry that it had to be over me. Later, after they all left, I got a little affected, too, for a long time over that. I knew that this was probably the one and only time my father would ever come to Guatemala on such a trip, and it seemed unfair that I couldn't be with him, and someone else would show him around in my place.

I arrived in my village late one afternoon ten days later wearing a forty-five pound full body cast, and my dad and all of the visitors except John, flew back to Minnesota early the next morning. That evening, though, something extraordinary happened.

"Here lay on this cot," I was told as I entered the house. "We put the cot here in the large room for you." I could only be upright for a few minutes at a time at this point. Soon after I arrived, people began arriving.

"We fixed the hole in the roof," someone told me, pointing up where I had fallen. It was one of the men who helped pick me up after my fall.

Others were arriving, too. Many had carried bags of pine needles down from the mountain and began spreading the pine needles down on the tile floor.

People came until there were a couple of hundred native people there. They came from everywhere in the village and they filled up our house. They carried food with them, too.

Soon I heard singing… softly at first, then louder with everyone joining in. I didn't know the songs, but I recognized the melodies that we often sing in church. And they took turns reading from their book of scriptures. They came to pray for me!

"Can we gather around you and pray for you?" One of the women asked.

"Yes," I responded, "that would be good."

"Can we lay our hands on you as we pray?" asked a man

named Michael.

"Yes, please do," I answered.

So, they gathered around me where I lay on my little cot, laid hands on me, and began praying. I think my body was almost completely covered with brown hands. And they began...

It felt like they had plugged me into an electrical socket!

Things were happening inside of me. Something was going up and down and around inside of me. It was a curious thing... it was wonderful! It felt like a fire that didn't hurt.

"I think I'm being healed," I thought. I got a glimpse of my dad sitting in a nearby chair, his arms folded, watching me surrounded with these native people, and a funny smile coming over his face.

Then they ended the prayer part and drifted back into singing softly again. I decided to stand up if I could, and so I did. That seemed to please them all. I took a step or two in several directions, shaking their hands and thanking them.

Then I lay back down on the cot. I was home again!

Then we ate together. They had brought corn tortillas and whipped avocados and an unusual white drink they make from rice.

Two weeks later I figured out how to get in and out of my jeep wearing my turtle shell. I was pretty clumsy. One of those times I started the motor up and tried driving around the roads near our house. I couldn't bend or turn around, but I could drive! I still got tired pretty fast, although within a week I was driving around the mountains again.

But, I stayed off the roof for the time being.

Chapter 12

Baskets of Plenty

"One of our biggest problems," said one of the teachers, "is that the children in our classrooms have a lot of headaches and can't concentrate."

"Are they getting any breakfast?" I asked. All of the teachers at our meeting knew the nutrition problems of the children. They needed to eat right in order to study well.

"The children are in this condition," said another of the teachers, "because they not only don't get breakfast, they don't get any supper either."

"So, the children are hungry." I said. There was a general agreement that the children were not getting the protein and vitamins they needed to concentrate and learn.

This was the beginning of a more holistic vision that came about in working with so many children. We never guessed at the magnitude of what was to be done when we began. The part about working with these lovable children was appealing. That part we liked.

We only wish we had counted them first...

We learned that education consisted of more than schools and books. "What would you think about building a kitchen at each of the schools?" I asked the teachers.

"Where would we get the food to feed about two-thousand children every day?" asked someone.

"Well, I don't know where the food would come from," I said, "but if we don't keep the children healthy, the education you teachers work so hard to give them will be wasted."

We built kitchens at eight of the schools where our children attend. We hired a cook for each school. Two or three of the mothers helped each morning on a rotating schedule at each kitchen.

I took some visitors around to see the lunch program one

morning. "I carry a large plastic cup in my jeep in case I visit a school during their lunch period," I said to the visitors, "then I have a cup of fortified oatmeal with the children."

"What does it taste like?" asked one of the young ladies.

"Well, it's kind of good," I answered. "They cook up a thing we call 'fortified oatmeal' by using powdered milk from the USDA, a very high protein beer by-product, and rolled oats that is donated from Holland."

"A beer by-product?" asked one of the young men. "Does it taste like beer?"

"No, It's not like beer," I said. "It's a fine white high protein powder we mix with the oatmeal. We also put sugar in it that we get from the sugar cane processors on the coast."

"This morning I saw children walking to school carrying a stick and a cup," said one of the visitors.

"That's how each child helps. They each bring their own cup for the fortified oatmeal, and a stick of firewood to help with the cooking fire," I explained.

"After the lunch is finished they take time for the children to brush their teeth. They each put some water in their cup and form a line," I said. "The teacher walks down the line with a tube of toothpaste squirting a dab on each brush. Then they brush and rinse with the water. The brushing lines give the teachers a chance to talk to the children about hygiene."

The distribution of food for the school lunch program took

place in we called the "basket room." It was a room with rows of long tables and seventy-two baskets. Venders would come there, and we would buy bread and fruit and other foods to fill the baskets.

That's seventy-two baskets of additional food daily. Here in this "basket room" they count out and divide the food and place the proper amounts into the baskets. Two baskets of food go to each of the thirty-six classrooms. The first basket had either tortillas or bread, and the other basket was filled with a different fruit every day. These baskets were a supplement for the cups of fortified oatmeal cooked-up at each school.

Two children come from each classroom at ten fifteen, to carry their baskets back for their classmates.

One day a problem arose in the basket room.

"We've got a problem today because we don't have enough wheat breads," said Melvin, one of the workers. "We won't nearly fill the baskets."

"And besides that," said Luisa, "there isn't half enough fruit today for the baskets. We're going to be really short on fruit, too."

"Go to the open market and get more," I told them, but even the open market ran out because we had already gotten much of the food from there. So we had to see what could be done... but they really were short of food and there was no time to get more.

"Just divide up whatever there is," we said, "and put equal amounts into every basket, and send them out with the children when they come."

Later that day I was visiting with a little group of teachers from one of the schools, and I said, "We're sorry that we had come up short on the food today."

"Short," they said. "We weren't short of anything. Lots of children had seconds today because there were extra. You must be mistaken about the food." All the schools reported having plenty for everyone and many had leftovers. We learned that it's not good to look too closely at some things.

"Today we have learned," we told our staff, "that we should stop counting things... In the future, we will stop counting out the food into the baskets. We will just do as well as we can and divide up whatever there is."

In the years that followed we just divided everything up whether there was much or little. In all that time, the classrooms never reported running short of anything.

We learned that we can only do what is possible, and after that experience, we no longer concerned ourselves with the impossible.

Chapter 13

Electrical Hot-Wiring

"Absolutely everything has some kind of a value, and can be reused as something else." This, I figured, must be an unwritten rule that applies to materials found in poor countries. I made a list of all of the materials that I found that were unused, or for which there was no present use.

My list had things like banana leaves, the sap from the Australian oak tree, the red coffee bean husks, cornhusks, the cooking water from corn boiling, etc. There were perhaps more than one hundred items on my list. I wanted to find uses for some of these things. To do this I would need a little workshop or a crude lab sort of place to work and do experiments.

We found a broken-down cement block building with windows along one side. It wouldn't take much to fix it up. I got a couple of carpenters, one who knew a little about wiring and electricity. We started by building a workbench with a sink, plumbing and taps. The water wasn't good for drinking because it was simply pumped up from the lake.

Then we put up some lights, added a propane stove, and some plug-ins here and there. When I went to check out the wiring I found that they had only used one wire leading over to some of the lights and plug-ins.

"This will never work with only one wire!" I thought, and walked over to flip the light switch. To my surprise, the light went on! "Now how did they do that?" I'm thinking. It was somewhat of a puzzle until I found that instead of a second wire… They ran the power along the iron water pipe!

That seemed a little dangerous to me so I asked them about it, and they had a very interesting explanation. They said, "Materials are very expensive and hard to get here in this village, so… we were just trying to save wire," they said.

A week later I rewired it, because I didn't want to get zapped.

I got all of the tools and materials together, and then went to shut the power off. The switch box was the kind that had a lever on the side one raises and lowers to turn the power off and on. The problem was that, this switch box ran the lights for several other places and a few homes as well.

Many people in this village often borrowed electricity from a neighbor because it cost too much to have an electric meter put in. The person who had a meter would "sell" electricity to some of his neighbors around him. The neighbors would simply run a cord over to the person's house with the meter. Others would then buy electricity by plugging into the second person's house.

Sometimes the electricity would daisy-chain to more than ten houses from a single meter.

"I'm going to shut off this switchbox," I said to Omar, the young man who was helping me. "You must stay right here and watch because someone might want to come and switch the power back on."

I was afraid that when I shut off this switchbox, someone whose power had failed down the daisy-chain, might come along and flip the switch back on while I am working on the bare wires. So that's why I posted Omar to watch before I turned off the power.

What I didn't know was that Omar knew absolutely nothing about electricity. He didn't understand that when a person works on the wires, it's bad luck for the wires to have electricity in them.

Electricity was a "mystery" to him and he never questioned it.

Soon someone, whose power had gone off, came to the switch-box looking for the problem. "Hey!" he said to Omar, "Why is that switchbox turned off?"

"Because David turned it off for a little while," Omar responded. "He said it would take about fifteen minutes."

"Well I need the light on in my little shop or I can't see to work at all," said the man.

They decided that that was a good enough reason. "A man has to be able to work," they reasoned, and abruptly turned the power back on.

Meanwhile I was at my lab pulling in some new wires. I

stripped the wire, curled the bare ends, and fastened them to the switches and plugs with the little screws. The last connection I made was to one of the ceiling fixtures. Then I went back up the stepladder to put in a light bulb.

When I screwed the bulb in the socket, it lit up!

"How could this be?" I thought. "Had I turned off the wrong switchbox?"

When I got back to the switchbox, I found my young helper faithfully watching the switchbox like I had asked him; only the lever on the switchbox was turned "on" now.

"A few minutes after you left," explained Omar, "a man came who couldn't see to work in his workshop so we turned it back on." After that hot-wiring experience, I always unscrewed the little fuses and put them in my pocket until I was finished working on the wires.

Chapter 14

Tappity-Tap-Tap

For several months I had to wear a full body-cast because of my broken back. The cast began at my neck and went down past my hips. I was able to sit, walk, and drive, but my movements were a bit limited.

The cast restricted me less than I had expected. In just a few weeks I was able to drive my jeep in the mountains again. I always wore stretchy bright striped pullover shirts. Now I just stretched them over the cast. If people didn't know I had a body-cast on, they couldn't tell.

In the out-back, I almost lost control crossing a small rushing mountain stream one day. I had taken off my shoes and socks to cross where there were large boulders about three feet below the surface. The boulders were slippery and the current was too powerful for me to maneuver well.

"Hey! I'm going to need some help," I shouted to my companion as I slid into the rushing stream. But he was across the river and too far ahead of me to hear.

I felt myself getting carried along too fast. I ended up about a hundred feet downstream before I got to the other side. While I was thrashing and struggling, sometimes under the water, I felt my cast crunch into a large underwater boulder, and that may have saved me from a broken rib.

My socks had gotten lost, but I had somehow managed to hold onto my shoes in the ordeal. "What took you so long?" my companion asked when I finally caught up to him.

"I wanted to take a little swim!" I told him. I worried about going back through that river, because the only way back to the jeep was to cross that river again when we returned.

When we did get back to the crossing, I was prepared for the strong current. "Make sure I get across the stream in case the current carries me away again." I told him. Even though I and my body-cast were soaking wet, it was a relief to be back in the jeep again.

Today was Sunday, though, and we were in a very large church in one of the most populated villages. They don't put any pews in this church because it takes too much space. People sit wherever they please covering the entire floor.

The children can run around, too, wherever they please.

"We figure that about four thousand people fit in this church every Sunday," Father Tom told me once.

So we found a place in the middle of this large church and sat down. People wandered around, probably looking for their friends, but slowly the place filled up and things got started. Everything settled down except for the children who kept churning about. It was time for the second reading...

"Klunk," something hit into me. It's hard to feel what it was through the body-cast. It was a child of about three or four years old.

"What kind of body do you have?" he must have wondered. It must have felt like I had a shell, like a turtle. A few seconds later I felt something again...

"Tap... tap..." it went suddenly. It was the same child tapping me with his finger. He was giving me a strange wondering look.

"Tap, tap, tap," and he was gone.

I was distracted now with wondering what the poor child must be thinking. I hoped it didn't frighten him or something. Maybe he thought, "Oh, I understand, Gringos have hard shells instead of soft bodies." That's when I felt it again...

"Tappity-tap, tappity tappity-tappity-tap, tap, tap, tap," it went this time. There were four or five of them now! He went to tell all of his friends, and then brought them all back so he could prove his story.

"How many friends does he have?" I wondered.

Then I realized that all of his little friends have lots of other little friends, too. ...And they did! ...And they all came tapping just like the first bunch.

"Tappity tappity-tappity-tap, tap, tap, tap," it went. "Tappity-tap-tap... tappity tappity-tappity-tap, tap, tap, tap." Every few minutes a new bunch came to verify the story! Off they'd run then, in a new direction to tell the news.

A year passed. It had been many months since that body-cast was taken off and almost forgotten. It was forgotten by almost everyone… except by the children in that huge church. They still came tapping every once in awhile. But now there was no cast.

They kept jabbing their little fingers directly into my ticklish ribs.

Chapter 15

School Desk Factory

Every time we built a new school, or added a few classrooms onto a school, we created a school desk shortage. I had two carpenters who were able to build tables and chairs and other wooden furniture that was needed at the project house.

"We need a carpentry shop," I said to Herman, one of the carpenters. "We need to be able to build the school desks and other things that we need."

"Why don't we build them right here in the corridor of the house?" asked Abelino, the other carpenter. "There is enough lumber here for at least two or three desks."

"Abelino," I explained. "We are planning to put more than two thousand children in school in the next village during the next year."

They both stopped in mid-stroke of sanding the boards on which they worked. They looked around at the little pile of boards, their crude workbench, and simple hand tools. "That's too much for us to do," said one of them. "That would take forever… It's impossible."

"Oh," I said kidding them. "If you worked really fast, and we put lights out here so you could work late into the night, and begin early before daybreak…" As I spoke a very pained expression gradually appeared on their faces.

"I'm talking about making a school desk factory!" I said quickly. "It's not for you two to do all of the work!"

"We would have to hire two or three helpers," said Herman, "and we don't have enough space for them to work here in the corridor."

They still didn't get it.

"There are plenty of young family men who can't find work… because they had no training. There are also many young men asking about scholarships so they can go to high school," I began.

"Why would we want to hire people who are not trained as carpenters? I ask you. You're not making any sense with this, David," said Abelino. "If they are not carpenters, they wouldn't have any tools, either. It's just not going to work."

With that, they both went back to sanding their boards again.

"A training school for carpenters that produced school desks," I thought, "and with a work-study program for students." In a flash of enlightenment, a new idea was hatched. We would try to solve several problems in one fell swoop.

"We will build a factory sort of place… and a school sort of place," I said thinking out loud. "I'm not sure if it should be more of a factory or more of a school. Maybe it should be more of both!" On hearing that, they probably figured that I had inhaled too much of the fumes from the wood sealer!

The amused looks on their faces slowly changed to more frightened looks as they realized that I was absolutely serious.

"You two will be the teachers of this training school," I said, ignoring their looks now, "and that means that you two will be in charge. You will help me by getting people to come and apply for a job here learning carpentry and building school desks."

"We would hire people who had no formal training and who knew nothing about carpentry. They had to have a large family to support. And they had to have been out of work for at least six months."

"That's half of the people in our village!" they said.

"Good," I said, "that makes your work easier. And the students who want to work and study… They must attend school and maintain near perfect attendance. They must work in the shop at least four hours per day. They can never miss school for work, or miss work when there is no school."

"Go now, and find people," I told them. "Find at least twenty. Tell them to come here tomorrow morning before seven if they want to apply. Put down your tools. Go!"

That was the easy part.

Getting the big saws, planers, and drills through the airport and onto the airplane was the hard part. Everything was over size, over weight, and hard to keep together. I paid baggage fines in excess of five hundred dollars.

Our factory looked a little like the average High School industrial-arts room. I did a great deal of safety training because of the large power tools. I had to learn the Spanish and Mayan words for modern tools, and when we didn't know the correct word, we looked them up in a dictionary.

We invented a new design for the desks we built. They had space for two children. We bought logs and sawed them up into boards by hand. We used the power tools for planning, drilling and sanding. We made a lot of noise in the neighborhood, but it was music to everyone's ears.

"This is our first desk," they said, when they had finally finished the first prototype, "We have to test it now."

"Two of you sit in the desk where the student sits," I said indicating the two heaviest men. It was really very weak and wiggly. I remember the men thinking it was magnificently built. I knew we had to get the quality better.

I explained to them what "quality control" was. When two grown men sat in the desk it was in danger of collapsing. The desk eventually broke when we put it on its side and applied a very little pressure.

Eventually we had a prototype that we couldn't destroy at all. I showed them how to use dowels and glue. How to use countersunk screws with predrilled holes filled with wood glue. We sawed out a thicker board from cured lumber, made better bracing, and added more screws of better length.

I ended up by calling our school a factory. We named it "Mayanwood" And the men were proud of their work. It was easier for grown men to say, "I'm going to go and work in my factory," than for them to say, "I'm going to school now."

These men became experts at using the power tools. They kept inventing better ways of doing things for which they automated their system of mass production.

They built more than two thousand school desks, as well as thousands of wooden trucks and toys for other markets. Not one of the school desks had ever failed or broken.

Most of the workers made a career of carpentry. Many of the men eventually went into businesses of their own, building beautiful custom furniture.

Chapter 16

Mountaintop Fish Pond

"The road up here to Santa Marta was a long, long climb," I said to Hazy. "My altimeter says it's seventy-five hundred feet."

"Yeah," he said. "It's pretty high alright." He had been there for more than twenty-five years. He had some of the most creative gardening projects I had ever seen.

"These are huge gardens!" I said looking at the rows and rows of vegetables and fruit trees growing as we drove by them, "You have a lot of workers out there... and it looks like they are doing a very good job."

"These are the new variety of raspberries that we're growing now," said Hazy as we walked through one of the garden paths. "These raspberries produce twice what ordinary raspberries do in the States." I mentally marked that spot by a large avocado tree, so I could return later and eat more of those raspberries. I love to eat raspberries. I used to sneak into my grandfather's garden and swipe handfuls of raspberries when I was a child. I can resist anything except a temptation.

Hazy had a wonderful gardening project that was able to produce a great deal of food for his high mountain village. "We have to haul some of it out to other village markets because we produce so much," he said.

Later we sat on the workbenches in his tool shop and talked for a long time.

"Are you a tool freak, too?" I asked him. He had been to my village and had seen our woodshop factory where we build school desks forever and ever.

"I've been trying to teach some of the young men about carpentry, but they would rather just work for wages," he told me. "People here get kind of lazy and don't know how to work for their future. All they think about is today, and having enough corn for tomorrow," he added.

"But you've got wonderful gardens!" I said. "I have never seen anything that successful, especially at this high altitude."

"No," he corrected me. "They're a failure, too." I couldn't believe he thought that those beautiful gardens were a failure. "Not one person in this village has a garden," he explained. "After all these years, people have not become independent and gone into business for themselves."

"How can we get them on their own?" he asked. "What can we do to make them more independent?"

"I have an idea," I said. "It's a little radical though. It would change lots of things about your project."

"Tell me," he said. "I need a fresh approach to this problem."

"Divide up the land of the gardens," I began. "Make plots that one family could operate and which would support them. Give them the plots that they now work on. Is that radical enough?"

Then I continued, "Say to them: 'Good and faithful servant, go and work this land. If you show a profit for three consecutive years, you will earn the title to this land. It will be yours forever.'"

Hazy began smiling and nodding his head at this radical idea.

"If, however, you should show a loss," I continued in my almost Biblical dissertation, "your land will be taken from you and given to the one with more. And you will be bound and thrown into the abyss where there is grinding and gnashing of teeth."

"Do I have to wait for three years before I can throw some of them into the abyss?" he asked. He was joking now, but I really think he eventually did something on that order to turn it over to the most responsible families.

Father Hazy had two churches twenty miles apart as the crow flies. When he goes to the other church to say Mass, he has to drive his jeep for seven hours to get there by road. There was a shortcut by mule trail that takes much longer.

"Lets go to look at my fish ponds," he suggested. "They're up past those big raspberry patches."

"OK," I said quickly. So, off we went to the fish growing tanks.

There were four tanks in all. They were built into the ground eight feet across and about sixteen feet long. One could see the small tilapia swimming about.

"We just built these tanks this year to have some fish production," he said. "The fish don't seem to be growing very fast. I think it's because of the food or water or something. We're trying to figure it out."

"What's the water temperature?" I asked one of the men who takes care of the fish.

His companion ran to the shack to get a thermometer, and when He returned, they measured it. "The temperature isn't too cold for the fish, but it's too cold to get a good 'bloom' on the pond," I said, "and I don't think they will grow unless the water warms up and there is a 'bloom.'"

It was a pretty high altitude to have fishponds. "It's hard to get a bloom at five thousand feet in our village," I said. "Here it is much higher."

"The sun is out during most of the day," said Hazy. "But it isn't enough to heat things up before it starts to cool down again."

"Why not cover the ponds at night to hold the heat in?" I thought aloud. "Doors could be built like those old-fashioned outside basement doors which flop open and shut and serve as a flat roof."

"That's a good idea," said Hazy, "and we could open them during the day to get more heat from the sun into the water."

"You could paint the insides of the doors white or silver, and prop them open at the right angle to reflect even more of the sun's heat in during the day. That might be enough to bring the 'bloom' on the water."

"And we'll close them when the sun goes behind the mountain," chimed in one of the workers.

As we headed down towards the raspberry patch, I looked back to see some of the workers beginning to measure the ponds with their tape measure.

Chapter 17

Christmas Forgotten

Christmas means doing half a dozen things at once. It always seems to arrive before we're ready. We're usually getting a new school ready with teachers, children, books, and supplies for the new school year, which begins here in January.

"Christmas will be busier this year with all that is going on," Betty said. "How will we get everything done?"

"I haven't a clue," I answered. "Wouldn't it be nice if everything didn't happen at once for a change. Christmas ought to be for families to have fun together."

That particular Christmas was even busier for us. It was a good thing we had some special people to pitch in and help that year. That Christmas our own children traveled to our project here in Guatemala to spend the holidays with us.

I think they enjoyed being together for the holidays, and soon rolled up their sleeves to help in doing the extra work that Christmas brings to the business of doing human development.

Everyone, even our native staff, helped with the flood of mail requests from friends in Minnesota wanting to send a little Christmas to the poor families with whom we live. We spent the week shopping, measuring children for clothing, planning, getting organized, making lists, ordering supplies, and packaging Christmas for hundreds of families.

Santa would have been proud of our Christmas list.

"Where are we going to have breakfast?" we asked the morning before Christmas. The four tables were stacked with plastic bags ready for loading into the trucks.

"We're going to have breakfast in the kitchen," Ana announced from her cookstove. It was very early and it was still very dark, and the roosters were just beginning to wake-up the village.

"The trucks are here!" said Dave sooner than we expected. That seemed to be the cue for the beginning of what would be a very long day. Suddenly we were loading the trucks, checking our lists, and gathering the personal things we needed.

We were bringing Christmas to the poorest village we had ever seen. We were prepared, we were coached, we had a plan, but frankly we wondered how we could get all of it delivered this last day before Christmas. Only a miracle would do it.

"I wish gift opening would last forever!" I thought when I was a child. That day I almost got my wish.

Our village office was like Grand Central Station. It was teaming with parents and children. There were children playing in the middle of the floor with their new little trucks and games. Workers had to step over, or around them. Others were trying out their jump ropes in the crowded street.

"Here is a list of the children who can't come today because they are sick," said Edy, one of the local workers. The list was a longer list than one might expect, and it was something we had not planned on.

"Pull those gifts out of the large bags and put them in the

back of the jeep," I said to Edy. "John and I can deliver them to their homes." So we went around, much like Santa, house to house delivering Christmas.

"Hold up your toy!" Annie would say as she took photos of tons of happy children with new toys and, "What do you have?" to mothers with blankets or other family presents as she took their picture. Betty and Julio were managing things, making sure no one was left out, and crossing things off their clamp board pages.

Then came the big surprise...

The day had finally grown dark, and it was late, and we were worn thin. Hours later when we approached our own darkened house in our own village, I remembered something that had been nagging at me in the back of my mind. We finally remembered that now we ought to have our own Christmas together too! We should have bought gifts. We should have been cooking things, and decorating the house. We should have planned something...

...We had forgotten our own Christmas.

"Get some wood," someone said. "Light up the little fireplace." We can still have our own Christmas together. Someone began making hot chocolate.

Soon the fireplace in our mountain village home was glowing from a warm fire. We made Christmas out of nothing that year. We stole things from each other and then wrapped them in whatever paper we could find. One of the things I received was a shirt that was in my closet yesterday. It came to be one of the best and most memorable Christmases our family ever had. We discovered that our joy came from sharing it first with that forgotten generation of children in that poor village.

It's true that Christmas joy is contagious.

It was good to be able to forget about ourselves long enough to experience the best Christmas ever. Although our thoughts were about Minnesota and snow and other family Christmases, we will never forget our special Christmas in the mountains where we had to be that year.

We kept a candle burning in the old church with the prayer that everyone gets the opportunity to experience the real Spirit of Christmas.

Chapter 18

Raggedy Man

Most families in the mountain villages rise long before daybreak. Papa always tries to get underway long before the children are up. Mama is busy getting the kitchen fire going.

"Wake up. Wake up children," Mother says to rouse them from their sleep. "You must all help with the morning chores."

The morning is chilly and so is the tiny cane house in which this family lives. The oldest girl is already dressed and is getting the corn dough ready for tortilla making. She takes the first stack of tortillas and wraps them in a cloth and places them in her father's carry bag, as he readies himself to leave the house.

"Go get more firewood," she said to her twelve-year-old brother who goes out to find more firewood in the morning darkness. The rooster crowing begins to rouse the family.

The smaller children always wake to the slap, slap sound of making tortillas and the smell of wood smoke drifting up under the tin roof. "Come on, get up," mama says again. "You must eat something and get ready for school now."

They rose and got dressed quickly because the mountain air was still cold. Soon they were out at the cement water basin to wash up with the cold water in the first morning light.

"Today might be different," Mama mused in the quiet darkness of the morning kitchen. They have moved three times this year, and once in the driving rain. It's easy enough to move... the family simply carries the bundles of cane, boards, and sheets of roofing tin, and the few cardboard boxes of their stuff.

They can carry all of it in three trips if it's not more than a few miles to walk.

Papa left the house early to go out job hunting. Soon they would be moving to a new location again... unless he found work soon. He went looking for work every day... then, later, he would go up the mountain to cut firewood so he can sell some of it for a

few centavos.

He knows there is little food, and soon the children will not attend school. Their raggedy shoes barely stay on their feet now. "What if one became sick?" he worried. "If I learned a trade, things would be better..."

Later Mama carried her wash-basket to the public water tank in the village square. She still hoped, "Maybe today something good will come. He will find work at the thread factory and then there would be money to rent some land, and for school."

"I have tried to find work everywhere I can think of," he thought as he walked from place to place looking for work. "If I don't find work today, I will at least come home with a little firewood from the mountain," he decided.

That was the day he came to see me, too, to ask for work.

That's how I know his story. "He needs to be trained in how to go out looking for work," I thought to myself. He has little training, little valuable experience, and no recommendations. He is a hard worker and he wants to be successful.

"What can you do?" I asked him.

"I can do anything you want me to do. I need the money for my wife and children because we are almost out of food," he said.

He looked like an unshaven raggedy-man. No employer would ever take a second look. He was looking for money for his family more than he was looking for work. He never told me what he could do.

"You can work for me in the afternoons building wire chicken cages," I said, "but you must spend your mornings out looking for permanent work."

"If you are not out looking for work in the morning, you cannot work here in the afternoon," I explained. "This is only temporary work until you find something."

But, first, we had work to do. We had to prepare him for job hunting. This first afternoon, we drove the little jeep around to his previous employers to get recommendations from them. We ended up with three very positive recommendations, signed, and on business paper. Then we found him some better clothes, shoes, and a haircut. This would help in the job hunting.

It did not take long. He was hired full time the next morning at the thread factory. Now there would be enough corn for tomorrow's tortillas, and soon maybe even school shoes for the ones who need them the most.

…And it was his job; he had found it. I may have helped point the way, but he was the one who finally won the job. A job is what he needed to regain his self-respect.

…And I probably lost a very good chicken cage builder before he even got started.

Chapter 19

School Lights

I have learned that there is often a community momentum that moves groups of people in one direction or other. It's like trying to start or stop a rolling boulder.

This happened once in one of the sections of a large village where we had been building a school. Building a school is usually very time consuming, and things often slow to a snail pace. The stone walls were up and the workers had been working on the rafters for a very long time.

While they are in the mountain cutting the timbers, the school site seems deserted.

"Here comes one," someone would shout. And we would see them come... five or six men, walking with a fast step; a long newly sawed four by six rafter on their shoulders. The men walked in unison, their shirts billowing in the wind, their arms swinging, the timber moving steadily toward the unfinished school.

"Drop it here on the sawbucks!" said the leader, "One, two, three, drop!" It bounced onto the sawbucks. It would be notched and hoisted later with a larger crew of men.

Eventually they got to the point in the building when they could see the end. That's when they got what I called "getting-done fever." More people came to help. More people came to watch. The excitement grew every day.

"The building is practically done!" they told me. "Today is Friday and we want to open school on Monday." They had a great momentum going and I liked it. "But come inside," they said to me, "we want to show you something."

"See how dark it is in here since the roof is on," they said. "We need to put some lights in here or it will be too dark to begin school on Monday." I knew that, because it was part of the building plans, but they acted like they had just thought of it. Now they considered it an emergency!

It wasn't an emergency. This community never had a school before. None of the workers ever attended school. There was no emergency last month, or last year, or a hundred years ago. There was no emergency now either.

"This is really community momentum," I thought.

"I don't want to discourage you men with some bad news," I told them, "but the truth is, we're out of money." This is the one thing that all of these people would understand, being out of money. "We've spent so much on this last part of the building that now we are very short of funds," I told them. I didn't tell them that we would have to drive our jeep back through the mountains on mostly fumes in our almost empty gas tank.

"It will cost four hundred and eighty dollars for the wire and fixtures," I was thinking, "and they could do the work on Saturday, and open school on Monday." After thinking it over a few minutes, I heard myself say, "Get the materials and we will pay the bill for the materials when we return on Monday."

So… it was decided. I could not bring myself to stop their momentum.

We drove back to our house across the mountain. When we pulled up to the house in the growing darkness, the jeep ran out of gas just before I turned off the ignition. "How is that for coincidence?" we asked each other. "We might have spent the night out of gas on that mountain road!"

After supper Ana, the house girl, suddenly remembered something. "I forgot to tell you," she said, "a letter came for you today." And she handed us the letter.

It was a letter from some folks we knew in the States. They wrote, "We know you are building a school somewhere and we decided to help." They sent a check for five hundred dollars! Could this amount be another coincidence?

They mailed it three weeks before, and it arrived by regular international mail. Regular international mail usually never even arrives! This must be some sort of an exception, too…

And finally, upon reading the letter, we learned that the man who sent the gift was a professional electrician.

Chapter 20

Mountain Wild Flowers

"Men don't carry purses," I explained. "And this is not a purse; it's called a 'side-bag with a shoulder strap.'"

"Well, if it walks like a duck…," Betty said.

"All the men carry them here, so when in Rome do as the Romans do," I responded quickly.

Those "side-bags" are really handy. I always keep a couple of them in the jeep. I wear one wherever I go, too. I keep books, money, keys, lunch, a Swiss army knife, and a couple of small notebooks, pencils, and more.

"I keep tools and even some car parts in there," I said. "So it's definitely not a purse. It must be a tool bag," I decided.

Once on a very hot day, we had to drive the jeep up into the mountains. It was late morning and movement in the entire village had slowed to a very unhurried pace. Dogs were sleeping everywhere; it must have been too hot for them to bark.

"Look out for that dog there," said Betty. "It's lying there on the side of the road." The dogs are very thin in these villages because they do not eat very regularly. "That dog looks like he is dead," she added.

The dog was dead. The narrow street forced me to drive, close to the dead animal that was left lying in the street. He was lying with some rocks under him, but you could still see the shapes of the rocks through his body.

"That dog was so thin," I commented, "that he only has one side!" Then, after we passed by him, when I looked in the rear view mirror, to my surprise, that dead dog resurrected himself, got up, and walked away. "He is a very thin *live* dog!" I said.

Soon we headed upwards, and as the jeep began to climb, I shifted to a lower gear. We climbed for more than an hour and a half. It wasn't long until we began to drive a little more level. Suddenly I noticed the temperature gauge was up in the red warning area. I pulled over and shut off the engine.

"It's still rumbling," Betty said. "What does that mean?"

"It means that we have to let it cool down before we can open the radiator," I answered. "And I hope that we haven't lost too much water, because there is no water up here anywhere." So, we just sat there and listened until the rumbling stopped. "It's going to be maybe twenty minutes before we can take a look to see how much water we've lost."

It was fairly flat where we had to stop. There were many brambling cactus growing about six feet high everywhere around, and big bouldery rocks were all over the place.

"Let's go and try to get some water out of that cactus while we wait" I said. "I've seen them do that in old western movies when I was a child." So, we dug out the Swiss army knife and tried to get water, but it only turned out to be a good way to kill some time. All we got was some sticky dampness, but no water.

"There are lots of very tiny flowers growing everywhere," said Betty, indicating an area full of them. "There are all kinds of them," she added.

I went to the jeep and got the thickest paperback book that we had. "Why don't you cut some of them with this scissors part of the Swiss army knife," I suggested, handing her the knife. "I'll put them in the pages of this book and we will press them flat and dry."

So she began cutting and handing me flowers. I got busy arranging them on the pages and turning a couple of pages every time I ran out of page space. We got so busy we almost forgot about our overheated jeep.

"It's really low on water," I said. "We'll have to turn it around and head back down."

"Can we drive it this way?" she asked.

"We can only drive it until it heats up again," I said. "Then we have to shut off the engine and let it cool down again." So we got in and I released the brake so it would back up in a horseshoe turn. Then I started the engine, turned the heater on, and we began our decent.

"Isn't it hot enough without the heater?" she asked.

"The heater is helping the radiator cool what little water there is," I explained. "If heat is coming out of the heater, we know the water is circulating and it won't ruin the engine." So she kept her hand where the heat comes out, to warn me if the circulation stopped. We went quite some distance before I had to shut the engine down again.

"Let's do some more flowers while we wait," I suggested. So we began cutting and pressing flowers some more. Our book was about a third full by the time we could drive again.

It took most of the afternoon to get down from that mountainside that day. It took many additional flower-cutting stops, which filled up our little book. Finally we saw the little bridge ahead that had a little creek running beneath it...

"Water!" we both said at once when we saw the bridge. I found a plastic bag in one of my "purses," which I used to get the water from the creek below up to the jeep radiator.

We learned to use our collection of dried flowers, too. We would dip a dried flower in white carpenter's glue and decoupage them on letters when we wrote to our friends back home.

"Then we'd place a note near the flower, 'Here is a real mountain wild flower that we picked for you!'"

Chapter 21

Turkey Rations

On the small farm on the edge of the volcano, there was a little flock of about forty turkey hens and eight or ten turkey toms. They were only laying a few eggs per day, and these were being 'set' under chicken clucks. None of the eggs were hatching.

"We're only getting three or four eggs every day from these forty hens," said Miguel, the man in charge of them. "Why do you think that is?"

"How much feed are you giving those turkeys?" I asked. "Maybe they don't get enough feed."

"Oh," he said, "I think they get enough to eat." He seemed kind of sure of that. I watched him sometimes when he fed those turkeys. He fed them on a rather sandy place where he scattered out only a gallon of ground corn for them. The turkeys went into such a frenzy to eat the corn, that they were eating lots of the sand with it. They were that hungry.

"Show me the feed you are using," I suggested. So we went to look at the corn that he ground up in a hand coffee grinder. "Only corn?" I asked. "Don't you add some concentrate?"

"No," he answered. "Concentrate is too expensive."

"That's the problem!" I thought. "They aren't being fed enough." A flock that size needed twenty-four pounds of twenty percent protein feed per day. Miguel was feeding them only eight pounds of eight percent corn per day. "No wonder," I thought. "These turkeys were on a diet!"

"They need concentrate with the corn," I explained, "and they need to eat all they want? They need a 'feast,' day and night."

"No way!" he said definitely. "I'm not giving them more feed!"

I could see that I had to explain it in more of a graphic and convincing way. So, I got a bucket with a dozen or fifteen eggs that were waiting to be set under a cluck. Then Miguel and I went and sat on a grassy place and I handed him three eggs and set the basket down.

"When you don't give the turkeys enough feed," I began. "There are very few eggs." At that point I took an egg from him... then I took another one... He was left with one egg. "The turkeys are hungry all of the time!" I told him. "And they can't lay any eggs." Then I took the last egg away from him so he sat there with empty hands.

"That's why your basket of eggs is almost empty!" I said, pointing to his hands.

"But . . . When you feed the hens all they want..." I said, handing him an egg, and then another, and another. "The turkeys go into better production because they are eating." At that point I reached into the basket and began handing him more eggs.

"Now they are healthy and laying because they are eating higher protein, too," I continued, reaching into the basket for six more eggs. I must say that at this point Miguel looked a little worried. He looked at his hands, which were holding all the eggs they could.

I handed him another egg, and another, and tried to give all of the eggs to him, but he could hold no more in his hands. So, I began putting eggs in his shirt pockets and his jacket pocket, all the time talking about turkeys eating lots of feed with concentrate.

"What do you think, Miguel?" I asked. "Do you want the turkeys to give you lots of eggs?"

"I want lots of eggs," he told me. "But I don't want to give them all the corn they want to eat." Then he added, "It's not fair!"

"Fair?" I asked, a little surprised by that word.

"Yeah, fair!" said Miguel, "My children can't have all the tortillas they want to eat, so why should these turkeys have all the corn they want to eat?"

I had forgotten the poverty factor. I was from a privileged world where man and beast alike lived in continual feasting!

I finally convinced Miguel that if these turkeys have a feast now, then they would produce so much that he could afford to give his children more of a feast very soon.

Within a few months we were hatching out more than one hundred healthy baby turkeys every week from the same flock.

We were using an incubator we had built instead of chicken clucks, and sales were brisk.

Then one day, Miguel and I were standing on that same grassy place. From there we could see all of the flocks, the new turkey feeders, and even the incubator in the egg-room.

"How much feed are you giving those chickens, Miguel?" I asked cautiously.

Chapter 22

The Church Bench

"Can I help you with something?" the storekeeper asked. I would always tell the storekeeper what I needed and then go ahead and buy it, or not buy it, and leave. It seemed pretty ordinary, but it wasn't ordinary at all.

"People sure are friendly," I'd think. I was totally insensitive about something that was happening during my interaction with the clerk. I finally noticed it once when a man who was standing in front of the counter buying something, noticed me and stepped aside. I looked at him as if to ask if he were going to buy something, and he motioned me ahead.

"Go ahead," they'd always say to me.

Then I noticed other people waiting too. They were waiting to be taken care of, but they always expected that I should go first. It didn't matter if it was unfair. They thought that I should be given service first, even if I had just entered the store and was out of turn.

Well, I'm just an ordinary person and I think that we should all take our turn. Besides it's their country, not mine, and maybe they should go first, and I should wait until last.

Once in a small farm church, the usher moved some people out of one of the pews so we had a place to sit.

"You folks can sit here," the usher said to us.

"We won't hear of it," I insisted. "Put that family back there." I said as firmly as I could. It was a battle to get them all seated in their pew again. It was a battle with the family, too, who also wanted to give us their seats.

Another time when we were in the great church in one of the most populated villages, they tried to give us special treatment, too. There were three or four thousand people there and all of us standing or kneeling or sitting on the floor. Pews took up too much space. We were just finishing up the Gospel reading when two or three men got up and walked through the sanctuary and out through the right sacristy door.

"What on earth is that?" everyone must have been thinking. Soon something large was jutting out of that sacristy door and moving slowly towards the altar. It looked like some lumber.

"The men carried something very large. Soon it was being carried past the altar as it slowly came out of the side door. I think the sanctuary was too small to turn whatever they carried.

The whole church of thousands of people was now fixated by this strange activity up front. Suddenly the men figured it out. They raised the thing up so they could carry it over their heads, and moved it over the top of the altar to maneuver it to where they were going.

It was a very large heavy bench.

They headed down the steps in front of the altar and disturbed everyone in the path they chose, walking slowly through the crowd.

"It's like a boat going through a lake filled with lily pads that move aside and back together again as a boat goes through with the water filling in again behind it," I thought as I watched their slow movement through the crowd.

It never occurred to me that they were bringing the bench to us so we could sit, while everyone else would remain on the floor. I first reacted by breaking out in a tiny sweat at my temples at the first thought of it.

"Oh no!" I'm thinking. Now they were coming straight for us where we were sitting in the middle of the church. "Who asked you to do that?" I yelled at them in my mind.

Suddenly there was some activity for us because we were now in their pathway, and all of us in that area had to rise and move out of their way. They set the bench right where we had been on the floor!

"Come," they said, taking us by the hands and leading us to the bench. "You must sit," they said.

There was no way out of this! We would have to sit on the bench. They were insistent. We could not refuse or argue with them, or argue the principle of equality now in the middle of thousands of people during the mass.

All we could do is sit and suffer total embarrassment, unable to lift our eyes and look into the eyes of the other people sitting on the floor around us . . . We had come to serve, not be served.

Chapter 23

JUAN COLLEGE

"Have some more tortillas, Juan," I said handing the basket of tortillas to the little old man who comes to our house for every meal. "Juan College, as we call him, never looks at me directly," I told the little group of visitors gathered for supper, "but he has a permanent smile on his face".

"None of these people read or write, do they?" asked Shirley who was visiting us for about a week.

"No, I don't think they do." I answered.

"Then why do you call that little man over there 'Juan College' if he is illiterate?" she asked.

"Oh, it's not a joke," I said quickly. "We're not making fun of him. He is one of society's outcasts, and we never question these people about their lives, unless they want to tell us." Then I added, "he eats with us because he doesn't have any money."

"We don't know his last name," I explained further. "We call him 'Juan College' because he goes to the high school in town and picks up the trash. Then he takes a small branch and sweeps the whole area down. That is his work," I said finally.

"Why don't you call him 'Juan High School' if he works at the high school?" she asked.

"Because the word in Spanish for 'high school' is 'college,'" I answered. "The people at the high school don't even know he works there, but we always thank him for what he does there. That's why I gave him that name. I think he likes it better than his real name," I said finally.

"Then," said Shirley after thinking about it, "it's not a real job if they don't know him and he isn't paid. So... why does he do it?"

"Because we know it," I tried to explain. "It's a matter of honor. 'Having work' in this culture is very important. It's part of who they are, I suppose. He invented his work and he does it faithfully."

"When I introduce you I say, 'This is Shirley, she is a writer for the *National Catholic Reporter,*' right?" I asked.

"Yes," she said.

"And when I introduce Juan I say, 'This is Juan, who works at the college,' and that gives him a place in this society, instead of being a nobody."

"What is a 'chu chu," asked Tom.

"A 'chu chu' is a dog," I explained.

"Well," said Tom, "you keep calling that little man beside you 'Juan chu chu.' Are you calling him a dog?"

"No, that's the nickname I gave him," I explained further. "Everywhere that this man goes, dogs follow him around."

"Why do dogs follow him around?" he asked.

"We don't know, but every time we see him walking on the street, there are five or six dogs walking with him," I told them. "I don't think he feeds them or anything, but they just love him for some reason."

"They are always different dogs, too," added Monica, "Sometimes I see him talking to the dogs as if they would know what he is saying."

"Tell me about that quiet person on the end of the table who doesn't use silverware," Shirley said, hoping for another account. "What is his story?"

"We know little about him, too," I said. "Except that his last name is Pan Hoch, pronounced 'pahn hoh,' and we have never needed to give him a first name. He doesn't speak any language that we know of."

"He doesn't speak any language?" repeated Shirley. "So how do you communicate with him?" she asked.

"By sign language, pretty much," I answered. "Watch this," I said. I got his attention and made a sign as if tipping an imaginary cup near my face.

He reached down, took his cup, and held it toward me as I filled it from the coffee pot on the table. Then he made a sign of rubbing his fingers together over his cup indicating he wanted Juan College to pass him the sugar.

"They say that Pan Hoch was the thirteenth child of a family and there wasn't much space in the small house where he lived," I told them. "When he was a little child he always slept outside somewhere and for many years lived alone in the mountains with animals and didn't associate much with other people. That's why he doesn't have good communication skills. He is only four feet tall and always wears the same scraggly clothes he's wearing now... and he carries that old bag of stuff with him everywhere."

"What is his work?" asked Tom, Shirley's husband; "what does he do?"

"He does something different every day," I answered. "But usually he takes our garbage down to the compost pile. He likes taking out the garbage because he always stops halfway there and cleans off any chicken bones that have something left on them."

I told them about last Christmas when all of these "street people" were with us on Christmas Eve, and we decided to give them gifts.

"You know how hard it is to buy for someone who has everything?" I asked as they nodded in agreement. "Well," I said, "it's just as hard to get something for someone who has nothing!"

"We finally came up with the idea of making him that bag you see there. That's a new old bag we gave him in which to carry his stuff. It's made of old pieces of material sewed together. We gave him that, and a set of new old clothes." I laughed. "Although it took him a very long time in the bathroom to change into the new clothes on that Christmas Eve!"

"Go check on him," I had said to the house girl. "I wonder if he is alright in there because it's been more than half an hour!"

So she knocked on the door and there was no response. Alarmed a little, she peeked through the keyhole and then let out a yelp!

"He is taking a shower in there!" she said laughing, "and now he is standing there naked trying to figure out his new clothes. God I wish I hadn't looked through that keyhole!" Eventually Pan Hoch came out wearing what was probably his very first Christmas present ever. We gave him applause and I think he really enjoyed the attention.

"He took possession of his new bag," I had announced. That was the good news. The bad news was that he had stuffed his old dirty shirt and pants inside and there was no getting it away from him that night.

"Where does Pan Hoch live?" asked Tom after watching him get up from the table, pick up the can of garbage and head out of the door.

"Oh," I said, "he doesn't live anywhere. He sleeps in different places. His favorite place is under the washing bench under our bedroom window."

"He sleeps outside?" asked Tom. "Wouldn't he rather be inside at night?"

"He used to live in the mountains, remember?" I reminded him. Then I told them how I could often hear him late at night crawling under the washing bench, and how I always get out of bed and give him a blanket, because there is no sleep for me knowing he is outside and probably cold.

One chilly night I had made hot chocolate for us when he came in the middle of the night, and while we were drinking it, one of the house girls heard us and got up and joined us with a cup, too. Soon Pan Hoch went out with the blanket I had given him.

"Why do you give him a blanket every night?" she asked. "You know that it's always missing in the morning. He goes out to those cane houses and sells it. He sells it to a different family every day."

"How much does he usually get for it?" I asked absently.

"He practically gives them away!" she said. "All he gets is a little money that other people, just like him, beg away from him to buy food."

"Well," I said to her, "I have seven hundred blankets that he is helping me distribute. What's more, he distributes alms to the poor on the side. That makes him an important member of our team.

"Besides, if you and I ever get to heaven," I ventured, "It might be only by his saying so, that gets us in!"

Chapter 24

Quiet Mountainside

There were always elements of danger because of the civil war that was raging during those early years. We had to walk a very thin line with regard to taking any sides in the conflict. Sometimes we spoke like politicians.

"Some of my friends are liberals and some of my friends are conservatives." We said in our political voice, "Us? We're for our friends." That worked for us.

"Let's walk through the village this evening," Betty said after an exhausting day. "And let's go out and sit on that beautiful part of the mountainside to watch the sun drop behind the volcano."

"OK, that's a good idea," I said. "Let's go right now because soon it will be growing dark." It was a very simple thing for us to do.

We stopped halfway there to talk to an old man who had a filing tool and was working on a small green stone about the size of a hockey puck. "You sure seem busy!" I said, as he looked up surprised.

"Oh," he said, "I'm making things to sell to the tourists who come across the lake in the boats.

"What kind of a tool is that?" I asked looking at the tool he was using.

"It's an old file and it works pretty good on these green stones. I wish it had a better point to scrape with," he said handing me the file.

"What are you making?" we asked.

"I am making ancient Mayan things to sell to the tourists," he said innocently. I don't think he knew the truth he spoke, because he was indeed an ancient Mayan himself.

Then, as we walked through that densely populated village, we noticed an unusual number of people in the streets. And as we walked on, we noticed that they were all going somewhere, just as we were...

"Where are all of these people going?" we asked. "They seem to be going in the same direction we are."

These ordinary village people were actually walking with us... and when we got to what we thought would be a quiet mountainside, we found the place filling up with people... The whole mountainside became a gathering crowd of people.

"I thought we were going to be alone here on this quiet mountainside," I said, feeling a little uncomfortable and self conscious because we seemed to end up in the center of what were now many hundreds of people...

"So," I said to a group standing nearby, "what is taking place up here?"

They explained something that seemed absolutely incredible to us... They said that all of these people... this multitude of villagers... knew that it was very dangerous for us to be out there at this time in this place.

"That's the only reason that we're all here," explained one of the men. "We just don't want you to be alone." They said we were safer if they were all there with us. They had actually encircled us and formed a human barricade of protection... against a serious danger unknown to us.

"We are experiencing a new reality here on this mountainside with these people," we said. "We are experiencing the reality of the Body of Christ." These simple ordinary people, much like ourselves, were standing against any danger regardless of their own safety.

It's a wonderful experience to be with others on that level... to be able to stand with them in their suffering... and sit with them and break bread with them. Even the cultural and national barriers now seemed to have been broken.

Chapter 25

A Barrel of Honey

One morning a small delegation of men came to my house with a problem. It seems that a fifty-gallon barrel of honey had gotten hard and crystallized in the barrel, and they couldn't get the honey melted again so it would flow.

"I thought everyone would know what to do about that!" I thought to myself. "Just heat up the honey and it will flow again," I told them.

But that wasn't good enough for them. They insisted that I come with them to see if I could figure out how to get that honey out of the barrel. So... off we went to this big granary where they also processed their honey.

There, in the middle of the granary floor, was the barrel of honey lying on its side, the middle bung facing upward unscrewed, and a light bulb about four feet above the barrel shining down through that open bung hole.

"See," said one of them, "the light is shining through that hole onto the honey and the honey is not melting at all."

"Well," I said with a grin, "this will be easy. Just raise the barrel a foot or so, then put the light bulb under the barrel and it will melt the honey, because heat goes up."

"No, no," said the other man, "if we put the bulb under the barrel, how will the light get into the open hole on top of the barrel?"

The third man looked at me as though I were crazy, "Besides, heat goes down," he said.

"No," I said gently, "heat goes up. Besides, you fellows are confusing heat and light. Heat doesn't always go where light goes."

"Just try it," I coaxed them. "We'll put the bulb under the barrel for a few hours, and you will be able to prove it." But they wouldn't hear of it. I think they were afraid that others would hear of it and laugh at them.

Their problem two weeks ago was that they had a corn sheller that ran backwards because the electric motor they put on it turned the wrong direction. They came for help then, too.

"There is a hard way to fix it, and an easy way. Which way do you want?" I asked them.

"We want the hard way," they said laughing. I opened the motor circuit board and changed the field polarity to make the motor run the other direction.

They fought me every inch of the way when I began to open up the motor. Their experience of taking things apart, meant never getting them together again. But I finally did reverse the motor.

"Now show us the easy way," one of them said. So I pivoted the motor up, and told one of them to take the belt off the pulley and put a twist in the belt, and I lowered the motor again.

"Why didn't we do that in the first place?" they asked.

"Because you said 'the hard way' when I asked you," I answered. Then as I began to leave, I heard the corn sheller start up again, and suddenly they were calling for me to come back again.

"It's still turning the wrong way," the puzzled men shouted over the noise of the motor, not realizing that now they had reversed the motor twice!

"Now it was different," they said. "This is not an electrical apparatus. This is about honey, and we know all about honey."

"So let me know when and how you get the honey out of that barrel," I said as a joke. Then I saw some hammers and chisels lying on a nearby table. I think they were actually going to chop the barrel in half to get the honey out.

"Just remember," I added, "heat goes up; it's a law of physics."

"Well, physics just works differently here," said one of the men. "In fact I'll prove it to you," he added; "just come with me."

So... he led me outside. "Put out your hands," he continued. "What do you feel? Do you feel the heat of the sun on your hands?" he asked.

"Yes, of course," I answered.

"Well! I was right." he said triumphantly. "Heat *does* go down!"

What could I say?

Chapter 26

Turkey Seed Stock

"Heat, ventilation, movement and humidity," I repeated. "There are only four things to remember."

Miguel repeated them again to himself. A minute later I saw his lips moving as he repeated them again. "I think I've got them now," he said proudly.

We were building an incubator to hatch the eggs from the chickens, turkeys, and the geese. The carpenters did a fine job building the insulated wooden frame of the machine, and now Miguel and I were putting on the controls and making the trays that would hold the eggs.

"What are these little wooden bars for, that run across the egg trays?" he asked.

"When we pull this lever, these bars roll the eggs and tip them over on the other side, Miguel," I answered. "Movement, Miguel, movement." I reminded him, "It's one of the four things." It was good that he was helping me build the egg incubator, so he would understand the workings of it so he could operate it himself eventually.

"This letter 'C' on the heat adjuster stands for 'cooler,' see?" I explained, "and the 'H' on the other side stands for 'hotter," I added. It was a confusing problem because "C" in Spanish stands for their word for *hot*, not *cold* as it does in English. "You have to just remember that."

That's why I wrote the Spanish words on either side for *hot* and *cold*, so they wouldn't turn the adjuster the wrong way. That 'C' and 'H' were embossed in the metal of the thermostat and couldn't be removed.

We finally turned on the incubator machine and began to adjust it. We soon had the humidity and temperature right. I had to teach him to read the thermometer very precisely, because we need-ed correct temperatures to one forth of a degree. I taught him to read the wet-bulb thermometer to figure out what the humidity was, too.

The next day we loaded it with the first eggs, pulling the lever and turning them over every four hours except at night. Miguel had to do all of the data readings and adjusting. We set more eggs twice a week. Soon the incubator was almost filled.

"The first hatch is coming off tomorrow," I said looking at the calendar data sheet we were filling out day by day. When the time is up tomorrow, we will have our first baby chickens, and next week we will have our first baby turkeys.

The children of the entire neighborhood came to see the baby chicks. "You can touch them, but don't pick them up," Miguel instructed. "It takes an extra week for the baby turkeys," I heard him explain to some of them. It seems like the hardest job for these children was to keep their hands off of those baby chickens.

"The clucks in their yards would never let the children touch any of their chicks," I thought to myself. It was fun to see the excitement on the faces of the children. Later, after we removed the baby chicks, we set another batch of eggs in the space where they had been in the incubator.

In a few weeks, it was time for me to return to the States for some business and supplies. When I left for the States, I left

Miguel in complete charge of the incubator.

When I returned, I had two hundred Nicholas first generation turkey-hatching eggs. We brought them as extra luggage in the airplane. I packed them in Styrofoam and wrote *Hatching Eggs* in both languages on the outsides of the boxes. Then we watched through the airplane window as the baggage men at the airport threw them roughly like the other bags on the luggage conveyer.

"We have to get the new generator set up and adjusted before we set the eggs," I explained to Miguel, "in case the power goes off during the twenty-eight day incubation period."

"How much gas do you think we need to have on hand?" I asked.

"We need to have a few gallons, at least," said Miguel.

"When the power goes off," I asked Miguel. "How many days is the most that we will be without power?"

"Oh, I think the most is three or four days," he answered. "But if the power is off too long, we can go and get gas at the station down in the middle of the village."

"If the power is off," I asked him, "how will the gas station be able to pump any gas out for us?" We finally figured we needed about twenty gallons of spare gas in case of a long outage.

I watched the incubator now very carefully. I had a battery alarm device in the house that warned me if the power failed. Twice I had to get up during the night to start the generator and plug the incubator into it.

The day finally arrived for the turkey poults to hatch. We hatched out about one hundred beautiful white baby turkeys. "These are very big chickens!" people would say because they had never seen a white turkey before.

"These are a new variety of white turkeys," Miguel would explain to everyone. "They will weigh about four times as much as the other turkeys do, and they will eat less feed." Miguel was very proud to show them to everyone who came to see our six cages of white baby turkeys.

"This is our nursery breeder stock," I said. We would be making an egg supply flock out of them. We were trying to have a flock of forty laying hens. They were our pride as they grew into larger and larger birds.

In the late spring, it was again time for me to return to the States for a break and to look for more funds and supplies.

"The cages are empty," I said when I got back. "So where are the white turkeys?" They must have moved them to another place.

"We sold them!" said Miguel excitedly. "We got more money for them than for those black turkeys. People were willing to pay a lot more money for them."

I couldn't believe it! Somehow he didn't understand that these white turkeys were our seed. He must not have thought about where we were going to get more of them. I was feeling angry, and he was thinking that he did a very good job of marketing. He was so very pleased with himself.

"You did well, Miguel," I said forcing a smile. "You did get a very good price for them." Suddenly we were back where we began.

Chapter 27

Corn School

"Ten bushels of corn per acre is very poor production," we said. "Farmers in Minnesota can get forty bushels without trying. They can get one-hundred and forty bushels if they irrigate," I added.

People here raised corn on the high mountain slopes. They took care of it all by hand. They had rain every day during the rainy season. And they planted in volcanic soil. "This will be easy," I figured.

"Let's do a corn school with some of the farmers," we thought. We'll make some charts and posters and try to raise the production. I employed the help of some very artistic Peace Corps workers to help make the teaching charts. I got some corn samples, soil data, and rainfall charts.

I was all set for the first class. Twenty men showed up in a country school open-air classroom. They were all great people, but they did not read or write.

"I'd have to go back to the beginning and revise all of the charts because they mostly had words on them," I thought to myself.

I mostly used the chalkboard for the first class. We talked about planting. We talked about fertilizing. They told me about all of the problems they encounter with their cornfields. It was a very good class for the first one, and they were very excited to plan another.

I had learned more about teaching such a class, too.

"I brought 'picture charts' this time," I explained to them. "I also brought notebooks and pencils. How many of you know how to write numbers?" I asked them.

All their hands went up. "You can copy the drawing from the chart and write in the proper numbers," I told them. They all opened their notebooks and became very large sized first-graders in my "corn school."

"Here is the first chart with bags of fertilizer. The 'P' on this bag stands for 'potassium.' The 'N' on this one stands for 'nitrogen.' This is how you mix it, etc, etc." And that's how it started... We had drawings of cornstalks, root systems, plant spacing.

And now they had drawings in their notebooks...

I showed them how to inoculate bean seed, so the plants would incorporate more nitrogen from the air to help the corn grow. I showed how to select corn seed from last year's crop. They learned how to get more humus into the soil to help hold the rain water, and where and when to place the fertilizer for best results.

I dug up old corn stalks and roots that I kept intact.

"See these healthy cornstalk roots?" I'd ask. "What's the difference between those healthy roots and these weak ones?" I questioned... and they figured it out.

The veteran high school teacher in me gave them homework, too. "For next time," I instructed, "bring in samples of the weeds that grow in your cornfields, we'll see what they are, and figure a way to get them under control."

They had a tradition of planting five seeds in one hole, then planting the next five seeds in another hole a full meter away. I wanted them to try planting the seeds more spaced-out in their rows. I took one empty chair and placed it in front of the classroom.

"Come and sit in this chair," I said, pointing to five of the men in turn sitting near the front. I always had to encourage them...

"We don't all fit on that chair," one of them said.

"How many here want them to try?" I asked the rest of the group. The group said they should try.

So they try... and I tease... "How do you feel on the bottom?" or "How do you feel left out with nowhere to sit?"

After they take their seats again, I ask them, "How do you think all those kernels of corn feel stuffed into one little hole?" Some of the men in the back of the classroom were laughing at the first five men... So, I walked to the back of the classroom where they were...

"You five guys, here is your supper!" I said giving all of them one single tortilla. "You wouldn't give one tortilla to your whole family for their supper, would you?" I'd ask. "Then how hungry do you think those five kernels of corn get, planted in one little planting hole?"

"Why do you push so much soil up against your corn stalks while they're growing?" I asked later.

"Because the corn starts putting out those little roots up higher on the stalk," said one of the men, "and we figured we hadn't planted it deeply enough."

Then I showed them an old corn stalk with the support roots sticking out so prominently, that I was able to stand it on the table. "These roots are to support the stalk from falling over when it gets windy," I explained.

They didn't believe me. They claimed that the higher roots meant that the corn was looking for more food, and by adding

more soil, they were also supporting the stalk more.

"No, no," I returned. "Those roots are like a tripod of support for the stalk! That's the way corn is." They still didn't believe me.

I had to try a new approach. "Do you think that God would make corn, and then make wind?" I asked them, "and not give corn a way to protect itself from the damage of the wind?"

Their heads began to nod in

agreement, "God would certainly give corn a means to protect itself." Now they believed me!

That was my corn school. And they all promised to try these new ideas. They each had a notebook full of pictures and some numbers that would remind them of what we talked about. I taught that course in four or five locations in those mountain villages.

"Our corn crop was great." They said the following December when the harvest came. Their production more that doubled or tripled for all of them.

"Are you going to do it again next year?" I asked one group.

"No," they said, "Next year we are going to plant four rows instead of the two rows we planted this year.

That's when I learned the meaning of the word "conservative!" They actually couldn't take a chance on their whole field because they might starve if my radical ideas didn't work for them, but they tried out all of my ideas...eventually.

Chapter 28

The Painter's Party

"The painters" are an unlikely group of men who became painters mainly because they haven't found their particular niche anywhere else.

"I don't think they particularly like painting either," was the general attitude of the people. The leader of the painters was the one not clever enough to get out of being the leader. "His idea of leadership is a lot like mine," I thought: "…find a parade and get in the front of it!"

He was a reluctant captain.

"It's generally understood," I was told, "that when there is painting to do, the painters have to do it."

"We have volunteers that can do it," I ventured.

"No! the painters have to do it," was the final word.

We bought gallons and gallons of paint, to paint the new family center that we had re-built. Painting was the last step of the remodeling. I can't see yellow paint today without remembering the painters. I think we gave them a run for it in the end.

"What's taking so long?" I asked the painter captain. We waited weeks for them to set a day to come and begin with the painting. They were not busy. They just waited weeks. So, I bugged them until they finally came one morning.

"Start with painting the pantry white," I said to them. I gave these five men a half-gallon of paint and they painted for two full days in the pantry, which was the size of a small bathroom. They also set a fan blowing out of the doorway so they could breathe.

"Paint the bathroom and shower yellow," I said handing them a half-gallon of yellow paint. That took two more days.

I watched them this time. They had a unique method of thinning the paint. They used gas to thin it. The paint was about one-third, and the gas was two-thirds.

"That's gas with a little yellow coloring in it," I thought to myself. I checked out this "gas" and found it to be kerosene. "That means that they will all just burn slower if a fire breaks out," I thought to myself.

A person could barely tell the change in color after the first coat. "It will take another coat at least," I thought. They put ten coats on the walls… five the first day and five the second day.

"I can't understand their work ethic," I explained to one of the carpenters. "Why do they work like that?"

"It's job protection," he explained. "They want to stretch out the work to protect their job," he added. "If they work too fast, they might not have work tomorrow."

"So, how do I stop them from putting 'gas' in the paint and needing to put on ten coats?" I wondered. I'll have to go to the meeting tomorrow morning and challenge them.

It was time to paint the big room the very next day. The big room was about fifteen times as large as those other two rooms put together. It would take them twelve work-weeks based on their past record. They would need ladders. They would need about six gallons of paint. I must get up early and go to the meeting.

There was a meeting every morning before the roosters crowed. All the builders were there, the stonemasons, the electricians, the plumbers, and the painters. They had the meeting to work out their work schedules, and for ordering materials.

I would make a short speech.

"These painters are marvelous workers!" I lied. "They have been working at painting our remodeled family center for the past few days. They do great work. And they are fast workers as well!" They were sitting there with funny looks on their faces, like they had me completely fooled with their silly "gas" mixing.

"So this afternoon," I continued, "I am inviting all of you to an open house at our family center. Come when you are finished with your work for the day. We will have fresh coffee, and we have ordered some cinnamon rolls fresh from the baker for you." The painters now began to squirm a little.

"Today we will paint the big room!" I said looking at them. "Stand up so we can see where you are," I announced. They stood up where they were sitting together in the back, and I began clapping and so all of the others joined in with a round of applause.

"By the time you all come at the end of the day, they will have completely finished painting the big room a beautiful bright yellow!" I finished. Then I sat down.

That afternoon almost everyone at that meeting showed up at our house. I'll never forget how they sat there, eating cinnamon rolls and drinking coffee in that big beautiful yellow room.

Chapter 29

The Master Craftsman

"The nuns in Rio Bravo want us to teach some of their families to raise chickens," I said to Pedro. "That's why we have to go down to Rio Bravo, which is two hours down the mountain on the coast."

"It's going to be hot down there," I said as we loaded up cages and feeders and things in the back of the jeep.

"Why is it going to be hot down there?" asked Pedro who had never been off of the mountain. "Because it's at a lower altitude," I began. "At sea level it's always hot... even when it's raining." He would have to experience being there for a day to understand it better.

One hundred degrees was usual there. Some days when we were there, it got up to one hundred and twenty degrees at midday. "Isn't it difficult working in that kind of heat," I asked the sisters who lived there.

"Oh, we're accustomed to it," said Sister Mary Francis. "This is actually one of our cooler days! At least there is a little breeze today, where yesterday there was no relief at all."

Half of the houses in this village were of old wooden boards or corn canes, and the rest were bamboo. One of the three families we brought chickens for, had a house built of bright yellow bamboo.

"Maria! Maria!" I shouted as I rattled the broken-down gate leading to their house. "This gate hasn't moved for years," I said to Pedro pointing to the vines growing through it. We waited for an answer . . . "Maria! Maria!" I repeated a little louder.

Then we saw a face looking out of the doorway. It was a thin face with a thin unshaven wispy beard. His hair was scraggly too, and combed with an eggbeater. "He is so thin," I thought, "he probably hums when the wind blows!"

"My name is Lucas," said the wiry man who came out of the house to bring us in. The children were beginning to surround us, too. "This is Miguel, and Little Lucas, and Maria," he was saying. We were shaking hands with them all and saying our names, too. His wife, Marta, was coming towards us from their cement washing-basin, wiping her wet hands and greeting us, too.

After all of the greetings, hand shaking, and smiling, I said, "We've come to help get you started growing chickens so you can make some money… Unless you don't need any more money…" I added laughing.

"We're so poor," said Marta smiling, "that our cockroaches have to go to the neighbors to eat!" Marta had a wonderful sense of humor, although I soon learned that she was probably right about the cockroaches going elsewhere to eat. I learned that she was the one in charge of this family as well.

"So, first we have to go and get some bamboo cut," said Pedro. "Lead the way to where the bamboo grows." Off we went through the high grass of the hotlands looking for bamboo. It wasn't long before we were headed back with bamboo bending and bobbing over everyone's shoulders as we walked along.

Lucas had not worked for eight years. He had lost his job and could not find another. He was unschooled and unskilled and could only do manual labor. The sister had said he had "a chronic illness and could not do heavy work." Our plan for him was not only to have him raise chickens, but to build cages out of bamboo at his home, and sell the cages. That would be fairly light duty work for him.

"Building cages," I explained to Marta, "would bring in more than forty dollars each week. That would be plenty of money for food and sending all of the children to school. He can manage it, and the whole family can work together to get the cages built and sold."

After about fifteen minutes of everyone cutting and splitting the bamboo into long strips to use for the cages, Lucas was nowhere to be found. "What are you doing there in the hammock?" I asked him when I found him on the other side of the house. "Why did you stop helping with the cage?" I asked.

"There are too many working there," he answered. "You don't need all of us working at the same time." I concluded that he was just lazy.

"You have to help; otherwise, how will you learn to make the cages?" I asked.

"The children can do it," was his best answer. He had chronic laziness, I thought.

"Come on," I said as I rolled him out of the hammock. "If you won't help, we are going to take all of our stuff and leave. We will go where people are willing to work with us."

So he came back to work. "I can't saw the bamboo because the saw is grabbing," he complained; and, "I can't split the bamboo because it's too slippery." Then later he said, "My fingers hurt when I wrap the wire around the cage joints." Lucas ended up mostly standing around watching the rest of us work. Then suddenly he was gone again.

There he was in the hammock again! This time he had three-year-old Maria with him and he was pulling on a little rope to make the hammock swing gently. "I have to give Maria her nap," he announced as I approached.

"No," I said sternly. "I'll give Maria her nap." I picked up Maria, saying, "Come with me, Lucas, because your sons need you." Then we walked back to the other side of the house where the cage was being built. "Get a hammer and a butcher knife," I said to him with as much authority as I could, "and teach your two sons how to split the bamboo... Go!"

He returned in a minute with a big knife and a hammer. "Put the knife here, I indicated with my free hand, and tap it down through the bamboo with the hammer." He did so, and a perfect strip of bamboo popped off as if by magic! It surprised me.

"How did you do that?" I asked

"I don't know," he responded, "I just did this..." and he did it again just as easily, and looking sort of surprised, himself, at the perfect strip that popped off.

"Now teach your sons," I said and off I went to the hammock to put Maria to sleep. It wasn't long and she was asleep.

When I returned there was a buzz of industry. Lucas was now the master craftsman, showing his sons the correct way to wrap the wire to make the lattice for the cage. His change was dramatic.

When the cage was finished we put the day-old chicks inside and they filled the water jug and a small feeder. No heater was needed in this hot climate. I gave all of the instructions to Lucas now, on how to mix the feed and take care of the birds.

"Now you children have to help your father with this project," I was saying to all of them before we left. "And if your father decides to build another cage, you have to listen to him and do what he says."

Lucas was now standing a little taller than before. Then I told him that if he builds any cages of the same quality, I would pay him twenty dollars for each one when we come back. Then after much shaking of hands and some hugs for the little ones, we were finally ready to leave for the highlands and some relief from the heat.

Before we left in the jeep, we gave some penny balloons to all the children from the bag of them that I kept in the glove compartment. "Hand me one of those balloons," I said to Pedro.

I blew only a little air into the balloon, tied it, gave it back to Pedro, and said, "I'll let the mountain put the rest of the air in it. Keep an eye on it." Sure enough, when we climbed back up to our village on our mile-high mountain, the balloon was huge from the difference in air pressure. It would have been easier just to say, "Magic!" rather than to try and explain it to Pedro as I did.

When we returned to Rio Bravo a week later, there was a surprise waiting for us there. When we stopped at Lucas and Marta's gate, they and the children came running to greet us. We inspected the cage filled with chickens. It had been well-attended and clean. I quizzed the children about the caretaking, and they answered all of the questions correctly.

Then Lucas led me to the other side of the house where he had built a new cage. "That's amazing!" was all that I could say. "That is indeed a perfectly built cage!" I said to him. I sent Pedro to the jeep to get one of the wooden cage nameplates. These were little three-by-three plywood nameplates with a small hole drilled in each corner for attaching them to the cage.

I gathered the whole family around to the back of the house where the new cage had been built. "This is indeed one of the very best cages I have ever seen!" I began, "and for this reason I'm going to put my nametag on it." At that I wired the little painted tag onto the cage with the name "David" and underneath was printed the name of the project and the cage serial number.

"I only put my name on the cages that pass my personal

inspection," I said. Then I took out a crisp twenty dollar bill, snapped it a few times, and handed it to the child next to me to pass it from one to another and finally to their father on the other end of the cage. "And this, best-of-all cages, deserves a premium!" I announced, and got a five-dollar bill, and snapping it, passed it the same way to this reformed, wispy-bearded man.

I noticed another unfinished cage setting nearby, along with a huge pile of bamboo. Everyone was simply beaming as we drove away.

We arbitrarily popped in a week and a half later . . .

"Lucas is dead!" was the only word. The house was in turmoil because Lucas had died only a half hour before we arrived. They had sent for the sisters, but they had not yet come. The neighborhood was gathering. I went into the house to check this unbelievable story, and indeed he was dead. Instead of a happy celebration, we were at a funeral.

The local laws indicated that we had to have him in the ground by the end of the day. I ended up helping to dig a grave that day in the sweltering heat, instead of enjoying another happy ending for this family. Marta told me privately that Lucas couldn't stop telling everyone about his "good friend" David, and then he would show everyone the nameplate on the cage. She said that he had become a different person with his respect and pride regained again, after eight years of feeling like nothing.

"That's how I'll remember him," she said. "And that's how all of the children will remember him, too." Then she took me back around the house with the children and showed me two more new perfect cages that he had built.

I gathered the children together and told them that the best way to remember their father's legacy was to keep building the cages just as he had taught them, and to sell the cages, which would provide for their needs in their father's absence.

"He used the money from the first cage to buy me a pair of shoes," she told me with teary eyes later. "I haven't had shoes for a number of years," she added. Then she explained that the rest of the money was spent on the things needed to get the children back into school, and that he had not spent one cent on himself.

"That was the first money he had earned in eight years!"

Chapter 30

The Blanket Loom

"So, what's the surprise going to be today?" I often ask, because there are days when I begin doing a thing in the morning, but then by mid-afternoon everything changes... and I end up doing something completely different.

Something like that happened one day as I and a couple of the carpenters headed out to some villages to look for a place where we could either buy some lumber that we needed, or buy some logs we could saw into lumber. We had been getting our lumber from Juan Garcia, who lives in a small village halfway up the mountain. He was very difficult to deal with.

He was difficult to find, too. There were eight Juan Garcias in his village alone, and there were many, many other villages, each with many Juan Garcias.

He could be depended on for three things. He would never come on the day he said he would come, he would never bring the right sizes or thickness of lumber we had agreed upon, and he would never have the same price that we had agreed upon.

"We have to ask for the wrong stuff and tell him to bring it on the wrong day for him to get it right!" we often joked.

Whenever he came to bring us lumber, he would come at suppertime so as to get a free meal and enjoy some bantering conversation. He was a good guy and he liked stories, being himself a teller of tall tales.

"These stories you tell of driving a pickup on a frozen lake and chopping a hole in the ice and then catching fish through the hole," he said laughing and shaking his head, "are the best lies I've ever heard." He was of the opinion that I was the greatest liar that ever lived. He shouldn't have encouraged me...

"It gets so cold in Minnesota," I said once, "that our words freeze when we say them, and then the words fall on the ground and begin to pile up."

"The words really pile up?" he asked seriously.

"You've got that right!" I continued. "We have to take them inside the house and heat them in a frying pan to hear what we're saying!" He was looking intently at my face so as to detect some glimmer of a telltale grin.

"There is a law there that if you leave your truck idle, you have to pick up all of the frozen exhaust from behind the truck and throw it beside the road before you leave, so other vehicles don't run into your frozen exhaust and dent their cars…"

"That story is probably a lie!" he said.

"I'd rather tell a story one-hundred different ways," I told him, "than ever tell a lie!" And that's the way we sat around the table, putting off unloading his pickup truck full of lumber as long as we could.

Today we were looking somewhere else for lumber, because Juan Garcia could not deliver the kind of lumber that we needed. We found another village much farther up the mountain where we could buy lumber.

It was a little community where the people cut timber and raised sheep. It was a poor community where the people struggled a great deal and worked hard for their daily bread.

"We're getting a very low price for our wool," said Tomas and his wife, as we sat with them in their humble wood house and had some coffee. "Sorry about the coffee, too," said Tomas' wife. "We can't afford coffee, so we have this," indicating a jar of black powder. It was corn that was toasted black and ground up and used like coffee.

"We need a better market for our wool, but the buyers pay us as little as they want," said Tomas. Then he asked, "Where else can we sell it?"

"Why not use it yourselves by making something out of it?" I asked, "How much wool do you have?"

"We've got quite a bit now because we haven't sold it yet," his wife said, pointing to several large bags piled up and covered on the outside porch.

"Couldn't you make blankets?" asked one of the carpenters who came with me. "I think it would be easier to sell blankets than the wool."

"You would get more money because of the work of weaving it," said the other carpenter. "So, why not learn to weave. That would be something the whole family could help with when you're busy cutting timber."

"We could learn," said Tomas, "but we could never afford to buy a loom." That was the dawn of a new plan. It would also be a new challenge for my carpenters, and an even larger challenge for this poor family.

The carpenters got out pencil and notebook and began making a rough estimate of the materials needed to make a large blanket loom. I got samples of the wool so I could get it graded and get the necessary cards and spinning devices to make a wool thread. There was a woman in another village who knew how to spin wool thread. I knew a man in yet another village who operated a small loom. These would be the teachers.

There was an exciting energy in the air. There was a hustle and bustle there, even in our voices. Our search for lumber was now almost forgotten.

"Here is a list of the lumber materials we will need," said one of the carpenters handing Tomas the list. "Cut it out of the best material and make sure it is dry when we return. It will take two days for us to build the loom, and we will return in two weeks to construct it."

It was months before the first blankets came off the new loom. I bought the first ones and gave one to each of the carpenters. There were some problems that were soon corrected.

The weavings had to be tighter and this made the blankets nice and thick. The loom had to be adjusted as it got used. This also gave the weaving more dimensional stability.

"We want to make designs on the blankets," said Tomas and his wife, "but we don't know how to dye the wool." The blankets were just wool-colored blankets up until now. They thought they would sell better if there were some way to weave in designs to make them more interesting.

"Why not use the black wool from the black sheep for the design instead of selling the black wool, and use the regular wool for the blanket itself," I suggested.

"Yes," they said, "that would be a lot easier than dying it!" And they eventually used some of the black wool to make a short black fringe around the outside of the blanket as well.

They made some very attractive designs and soon had a fairly good product to sell. The last we heard, they went out and bought an old pickup truck for their lumber and blanket business. They were doing well.

They always delivered our lumber in the sizes we needed, and on the day upon which we had agreed.

Chapter 31

Little Rosa Is Sick

The humidity was rising and the mid-day heat began to soar upwards without mercy.

The back seat of our little red jeep was filled with boxes of pharmaceuticals for the little pharmacy that was run by a small group of nuns in Rio Bravo in the hotlands down on the coast. We often supplied them with the medical things that they needed to serve the people of that vicinity.

We also had trained quite a number of poor families there to raise chickens and do carpentry or gardening in an attempt to raise their income.

"Why are those people over there on that back street waving to us?" we asked ourselves. We were driving through the back streets of the village on our way to the pharmacy, and some people were waving and trying to get our attention from one of the side streets. "Why, that's where Mirna lives with her children," we said.

She was one of the widows we had been working with to grow a large garden and raise cages of chickens. We quickly swung the jeep around and pulled up near their house made of wood slabs from a nearby sawmill.

"What is it?" I asked the people in the street. "Why do you want us to stop?"

"It's little Rosa," they said. "She is very, very sick."

She was the little girl from the family with whom we had been working, who lived in the large slab house. We knew her and the rest of her family very well. She was just a sweet innocent child about four years old.

"She may die if she doesn't get medical help," said a woman from the neighborhood. "I've seen this before, and she is not getting any better."

In the house I found Mirna, the child's mother, sitting by the child's bedside. The child was lying on a cot with a mattress of woven cornstalks covered with a blanket. I could read the worry in the eyes of the mother.

"How long has little Rosa been sick?" I asked quietly.

"It's been three days now since her fever got really high," she said. There was a waver of hopelessness in her voice.

"Has she had any medicine?" I asked, thinking about the irony of having the back seat of our jeep full of medicine, and none of us knowing what would help her.

"No," Mirna answered, "we have no medicine."

"When did she eat last?" I asked, noticing that the room was filling up with people.

"She hasn't eaten for two days," she replied.

"And when did she last drink anything?" I asked as I looked at the child's pale face and observed her lying there a little too calmly. Last time I saw her, she was running and giggling.

"Nothing so far today," she answered, knowing that her answers were all the wrong answers, and it confirmed all of her worst fears.

"And the sisters?" I asked some of the others gathered around. "What have they said?"

"The sisters are not here this week," someone behind me answered.

I reached down and took little Rosa's face in my hands. She felt damp and hot. Her hands felt clammy and her eyes were closed. Her breathing was very shallow. People were looking at me anxiously as if to say, "Can't you do something to save her?"

I had seen children in better condition than this die. There wasn't a doctor for hundreds of miles. All I could think of was that maybe we could pray for her.

"Gather together the neighborhood community," I said. The room we were in was large and there were big windows that looked into their open yard on two sides of the house. "Someone should go and find a Bible for me to use," I said to a couple of women standing nearby.

We had to wait awhile for the Bible because very few in this whole village were able to read. That gave time for people to gather and fill up the room and the yard outside the two open windows.

Someone handed me the Bible and I began with something

they would know, "The Lord is my shepherd, there is nothing I shall want."

Everyone repeated those words in unison, "The Lord is my shepherd, there is nothing I shall want." And that's the way we finished that Psalm; each time I read a line, they repeated it.

After a couple of other readings, I began a prayer asking God to heal her of her sickness. "Lord," I began, "Little Rosa is an innocent child, and she is very sick right now. We are all here asking that you heal her of this sickness. Little girls are supposed to run and play and sing and shout. That's what you have created her to do. We know that you will heal her and we are all grateful for your willingness to make her well."

Then I said, laying my hands on her, "Thank you Father for making her well and taking away her fever. Later she will be getting up and want something to eat and drink. Then she will go outside to play because you have healed her. We just thank you and praise you for what you are doing for this poorest of your children, amen"

And that was all that we could do.

Something was annoying me as I talked to some of the people during the next few minutes. Something was bugging me in the corner of my mind. Then I realized what it was! There was a little boy there, tugging at my shirt! What's this little boy doing that for?

"What?" I said kind of exasperated, turning suddenly towards him. He looked a little shocked at that, and said something to me that I didn't understand. Then he repeated it to me.

"My mother is very sick, too," was his simple statement.

"Where?" I asked quickly.

"A block away," came the reply.

I quieted everybody down again and said to them, "We are all going to go and pray for this little boy's mother." Then turning to the boy, I said, "Lead the way, son," and followed him to a house about a block or so away. The crowd of people came and followed after us.

We found his mother with a burning fever, lying on a cot in their one-room house. She had been sick since yesterday with a burning fever. As soon as the neighborhood gathered around again, I began like I did before with something from the Bible.

This time I said, "Lord this woman needs to care for her family.

She needs to be well so she can feed and look after her children. We ask that her fever leave her, and that she is healed so she can walk to the market and go to the public tank and wash her clothes."

Then I laid my hands on her and continued, "We thank you, Lord, for restoring her to perfect health. We can see her going to visit with her neighbors and walking down the street with her friends. We see her carrying a basket of food home from the market, and working about her kitchen, making the tortillas for her family. For this we praise and thank you, Lord, amen."

At that I handed the Bible back to the woman who gave it to me, and said goodbye to everyone and soon left in the little red jeep.

We spent the rest of the day at another village farther down towards the sea. When we were finished there and heading back to our home up on the mountain, we stopped first to see the families in Rio Bravo we had visited earlier.

When we pulled up by Mirna's house, little Rosa was outside in their yard playing with some blocks of wood. She didn't remember anything about our being there in the morning. Her mother said that about an hour after we left, Rosa got up, her fever having left her, and wanted to eat because she was hungry.

One of the neighbors outside asked us if we heard about the woman down the street. "No," we said, "what's the story about her?"

"Well," the neighbor woman began, "she is well and walking to see her neighbors and going to the market and everywhere. She is just like she was six years ago!"

"Six years ago?" I asked puzzled.

"Yes," said the woman. "She has been in a wheelchair for the past six years, but since we prayed for her this morning she has been up walking all over the place!"

"It's a good thing that I didn't see that wheelchair!" I thought to myself. "I would never have had the courage to pray for her saying the things that I said. The faith of these people is a lot stronger than mine."

In all of the villages and occasions when we gathered the people and prayed with them for someone who was sick, we could not recall even a single incident, over the years, when they were not healed or at least greatly improved. We discovered the great healing faith present in these poorest of God's people.

Chapter 32

Jeep Coil-Checker

When there is a problem with the jeep, getting it fixed can be a real circus. Most of the mechanics here know less than we do, and some don't even know how to drive. Generally speaking, if they don't know what something is used for on a vehicle, they will remove it.

We brought cars down from Minnesota that had the little electric plugins hanging somewhere out of the grill to preheat the coolant for better starting in winter. This they could never understand.

"Isn't the idea of coolant to cool the engine?" they'd ask with a puzzled expression.

"Yes, but…" I'd begin, but no explaining ever cleared up the matter. So off it came. They never understood why you needed brakes on all four wheels! Two or three maybe, but not all four… how extravagant!

Once I ran out of gas in the mountains, and couldn't turn on my spare tank, which I always kept full of gas. The switching valve seemed to be missing. I crawled under the jeep and found to my amazement that the spare tank had also been removed!

"I needed it for another guy's car!" was the explanation.

"You have never used your extra gas in all the time you've been here," he continued. "But someone else really needed that gas tank!" I think the word for this is "involuntary sharing."

The rule for four-wheel-drives is that one goes down the mountain in the same gear that you climbed up the mountain. That keeps the vehicle from becoming a runaway going down the mountain. But one day on a rare flat piece of road I could finally shift into high gear, but it was like freewheeling. There was nothing there… It was like being in neutral.

When I asked my mechanic to fix it, he pointed to my gear wheel lying near his house. It had become his flagpole stand with a small Guatemalan flag on a small pole flapping in the breeze.

"You never use that high gear!" he said. "So I removed it almost six months ago now!" Maybe he was right. I almost never get to use high gear.

Once, when my jeep wasn't running very well, I changed the spark plugs, the points, and I adjusted the carburetor. I got the idea that it must be the coil that was failing. So off I went to my mechanic's shop.

"Do you have a coil checker?" I asked.

"Yes I do," came the answer.

"So… How much does it cost to check my coil?" I asked, because one always has to be up-front about the price.

"For you, because we are friends, I'll do it for ten dollars," he answered. That was a pretty steep price, partly because his mechanic shop was a rustic open-air shop about half the size of the average bathroom.

"You really have a coil checker?" I asked, because it looked like he had only about ten or twelve tools. He had a screwdriver and a pair of pliers. He also had a very large pair of pliers that saved him the price of a set of sockets and box-end wrenches.

"Yes I have a coil checker," he replied, acting a little like I had insulted him.

"OK," I was desperate, "check my coil for me."

Now, the next thing he did was amazing! First he opened my hood and removed my coil, then he stopped the next jeep like mine coming down the road. He opened their hood, removed their coil, replaced it with my coil and had them start their car.

When their car started up all right, he put their coil back in their car, and finally put my coil back in my car.

"It checks out good," he said with a grin. "That will be ten dollars please!" ...I'll never forget the surprised look on the other jeep driver's face, too!

Chapter 33

Popcorn Sheeting

Construction boards and sheeting are really expensive here. Any kind of dimension lumber is very expensive, too. Most Plywood and particleboard is imported.

"Doesn't anyone here make any kind of building board?" I asked the builders, one morning at their early morning builder's meeting. "It's so expensive," I stated, "that most families can't afford to buy the construction sheeting they need."

"They use cornstalks for their walls," said one of the men, and they all laughed. "Cornstalks are cheap, and people can afford them alright," said another.

Later, I checked through my notebook where I had made lists of things around the village that are unused or are thrown out. "Some of these things could be used as raw materials," I thought to myself. Then I noticed something on my list the people called "goma" which was like a gum or pitch that oozed out of the Australian Oak tree.

I watched the children use it like glue to fix their kites last November when they all went kite flying. "Maybe this would work like a resin in bonding some other materials together," I thought. "I'm going to have to get some of that stuff… a lot of that stuff, and I'll have the children collect it for me."

Near a settlement on the outskirts of the village, there grew a large number of these Australian Oak trees. "Here are some plastic bags," I announced to the group of about twenty children who gathered around the big rock I was sitting on. "I want you to collect the sap and pitch from this kind of tree," I continued, indicating the tree near me.

"Are you Father Greg's brother?" came the first question.

"No, why do you ask?" I responded, wondering why the topic was changing.

"Because you look like him." Came the answer from

another of the children. They always thought all of us Gringos looked alike.

"I'll pay a dime to anyone who fills up a bag of 'goma' for me!" I said, quickly getting their attention back. "If you fill two bags, I'll give you two dimes," I added.

The bags were about the size that would hold about a pound of the stuff. "I'll come back tomorrow at this same time to buy the bags of 'goma' from you," I announced. Then I passed out the bags to them. Some of them even wanted two bags! They were excited now and ran in every direction to find the trees and climb up and fill their bags with goma for me.

The next day at the same time I went back to the same rock and sat there and waited for the children to show up. This time I had a pocket full of dimes! There weren't many children around. "So what happened to yesterday's excitement," I asked myself.

Eventually the children gathered around the rock and waited. I didn't see any "goma" bags anywhere. Soon there were quite a bunch of children gathered.

"How many of you have gathered a bag of 'goma'?" I asked.

No one answered. They just stood silently looking at each other, wondering, too, if any of them had filled a bag with 'goma.'

"Are you Father John's brother?" asked one of them.

"No, why? Do I look like him?" I asked.

"No," said the child, "But you're sitting on his rock! That's the rock that he sits on to rest every morning when he goes running."

"Don't any of you want to fill these bags of 'goma' for me even if I pay you a dime for each bag?" I asked them. Then I put the bags on the rock beside me and I reached in my pocket and pulled out a large handful of dimes and showed them the money.

It was like magic! The children disappeared and so did all of the bags. I could see some of them getting ready to begin climbing the Australian Oak trees as I walked away.

Next day I was back on my rock with the pocketful of dimes. When the children gathered, they still had no bags of "goma" that I could see.

"Didn't anyone gather any 'goma' for me?" I asked, waiting. After a moment one little girl slowly raised her hand, but I didn't see that she had a bag of "goma."

"Do you have a bag of 'goma?'" I asked her.

"I have at my house," she answered weakly.

"Go get it!" I said, "I'll wait…" Off she ran.

When she returned and handed me the bag, I handed her one of the dimes. It was amazing. The rest of the children's eyes were bugging out! They couldn't believe what they were seeing. I had actually paid a dime for a bag of "goma," a thing so worthless to them, that they couldn't believe it. Two little boys ran to their houses to get bags of "goma" and each received a dime.

Now there was a din of noise and jabbering among them. They ran off with more empty plastic bags in every direction.

"Now, I've seen that before," I thought as I walked back home with only three bags of "goma." "Tomorrow will be Act IV."

But I was wrong. There were bags of "goma" everywhere. Many of them had two bags. I bought "goma" until I was out of dimes. I went back for two more pockets of dimes and a wheelbarrow. The children were still waiting. When I finished, it took two loads with the wheelbarrow before I was done hauling the stuff.

It was time to concentrate now on making the sheeting that would revolutionize the building industry.

When I was a child, my dad always liked to make popcorn balls. He'd mix up the caramel syrup and put the popcorn in a giant aluminum bowl.

While stirring the popcorn with a giant spoon, Mom would pour the hot caramel syrup over the popcorn as my dad mixed it around with a large spoon. Then while it was still hot it could be formed into round balls or shaped into anything. As it cooled down, it would harden in whatever shapes a person had made.

That was pretty much how we made the first sheets of building board. Instead of popcorn, we used shredded corn stalks, peanut hulls, dried coffee husks, the fibrous stem pieces of banana trunks, and things like that.

"Pour a little more of the hot melted 'goma,'" I said to Pedro, as I mixed with the big spoon. "Good, now help me dump this stuff into the form," I said, as I motioned which direction to dump the tub. "It's like making the popcorn balls I told you about!" I said. "Only this time we're making 'popcorn boards'!" We flattened it into about a two-foot square piece and then pressed and hammered it until it was only about an inch and a half thick.

"We need something to make it waterproof now," we said after testing the board in a water tank. After one day in the water, the particles in the board began to break-up and swell.

Our second attempt was more successful. We boiled the "goma" down more, and added some raw latex from the rubber trees. "Let's sun-dry the piece of board now," suggested Pedro. "We can put it on the roof of the shed where the sun hits directly," he added. We used the whole weekend to dry the piece of board, flipping it over each time we walked past it. Then we sanded one side with the sanding blocks.

Early Monday morning I went to the builder's meeting. I laid my piece of board on one of the tables while I filled my cup with coffee and went about greeting people. These were strange meetings. There was no starting time, and no organization whatsoever. The meetings just happened. The men talked about things one on one, or in little groups sitting or standing around, but often they'd discuss things as a large group with everyone listening in and making comments.

"What is this thing you brought in here, David?" asked a couple of the men, as most of the conversations stopped and the groups turned to hear the answer. They had picked up the piece of board now and were looking at it.

"Pedro and I made a sample of the board we want to try using for building things," I answered. "We think it could be used as sheeting for houses or sheds or something. What do you all think?" I asked.

"What's it made of?" asked one of them.

Pedro went through all of the materials we used in making the board with them. Then he told them how we manufactured it, and tested it. It had an appealing look to it.

They actually laughed at the whole idea. They laughed at the word "goma" which sounds like the word "gomma," their Mayan word for "a drunken hangover." "You can get lots of 'gomma' in the streets the day after the fiesta," they laughed.

"This board will never hold up like wood," announced the woodcutters with final determination.

"It might not take paint very well," said the head of the painters group, and then concluded, "the paint will peal right off of it."

"It looks kind of nice without paint," said one of the stonemasons. "Maybe if we use this stuff, we won't need painters any more." That brought a roar of laughter at the expense of the painters. At least now they were laughing at the painters instead of us.

"So this stuff will never work for building things," I said, repeating their conservative conclusion.

"No, it won't work well because it's too weak," said one of the men, whose job was to lift heavy rafters in place. When this strongest of men, who was built like one of the oxen, said something was weak, there was no argument.

"It would probably be pretty easy to break in half wouldn't it?" I teased.

"It would break too easily," he said quickly laying it down on the table. Then I took out a five-dollar bill and laid it on the table with the piece of board.

"Whoever can break that board this morning, can have that five-dollar bill," I challenged them. Then I went across the room to refill my cup with coffee and got ready to sit back and enjoy the show. For a long time everyone tried to break the board, but could not. I think they had a lot of fun trying and laughing at each other in turn.

"Could a family make any money selling 'four-by-eight' sheets of this stuff," I suddenly asked, "having gotten all of the materials for free?" That caused a sudden change in their conversation.

When is the best time to gather "goma," they asked each other. "Is it during the rainy season or the dry season?" Some of them thought it was the rainy season because there was more juice in the trees then. Others said it was the dry season because the trees were dormant and the trees didn't need the "goma" then as much.

This argument lasted for fifteen minutes without a single logical argument on either side.

Finally they decided to put the question to the guy who was the "tree guy" who planted and cared for trees that he sold. He knew how to graft different varieties of fruit trees together.

"The dry season," he said with finality.

"Why?" someone asked.

"Because during the rainy season," he said authoritatively, "the rain comes down through the leaves and branches," motioning with his arms, "and it washes the goma…" He hesitated as he waited for an idea, the room hanging on his every word, "down and away!" he said, pushing with his hand motions 'down and away.'

There were no further questions, and all of the men nodded in agreement. Then the meeting ended, with the five-dollar bill still lying on the table with the unbroken piece of 'popcorn board.'

Chapter 34

Cement and Sherbet

A new Junior High School was being built in the center of the village. It was a large community project and many people were helping to get it financed and built. This was a very poor village so everyone had to pitch in and help. There were many volunteers, and they would give a few days whenever they could. A few people who had money helped financially as well.

"Get those mud boxes lined up over there!" Lucas shouted at some of the men. "A little farther apart," he shouted again, "so you won't get in each other's way when you mix the concrete."

"How many pails do we have to carry cement?" hollered Lucas to three workmen carrying stacks of metal pails. An inaudible number was shouted back to him. "Good," Lucas continued. "Put those pails there at the ends of the mud boxes."

Lucas was in charge.

There were over a hundred men who showed up at first light that morning to help. They would mix cement and move the cement with a bucket-brigade to the foundations and pour the cement by hand. Another line of men would also form a return-line to toss the buckets to one another returning them to refill with cement again.

The foundations were seven feet deep. The steel rods were all wired carefully in place, waiting for the concrete. The new school building would rise from these underground supports. Soon we could hear the shoveling and scraping sounds of cement being mixed by hand.

"Make a line! Make a line!" everyone heard Lucas shout. "We're starting on the east side on the south corner." There was a hustle of movement to find a place in the brigade line, or the return-bucket line.

"Watch out for those braces," somebody yelled. "Be careful not to move them." One could sense the greater authority of the regular builders over the men who only came to help for the day.

Suddenly there was a feeling of haste and urgency as the real work began. The first buckets were being filled and started down the line. The men with me, farther down, were pulling their gloves tighter as they waited, getting ready for their share of the work. In minutes the entire place erupted into work and action, including the buckets being tossed along the return line back to the mud-boxes. All you could hear for many minutes were the sounds of the buckets working their way up to the foundation and the tossing action on their way back to be refilled.

It was a brotherhood of workers. It was a bond of men who were acting as one machine getting the cement into the forms of the foundation. I was a North American, the man beside me was Mayan Indian, many were Ladinos, and still others were mixed. It made no difference because we were all brothers.

Soon there was a little talking here or there, and voices could be heard, sometimes laughing. Lucas had said that this work would take thirteen hours with these hundred men.

"Pace yourselves," he said to the men. "Work with a steady pace and you will drop less buckets. We will take our first break at ten-thirty. We will start at the first morning light, and we must finish just before the sun moves behind the volcano."

"We have worked steady for four and a half hours!" said someone sitting near me during this "ten-minute" break. "We are hot and sweating and that sun keeps beating down as we work without any shade."

All of the men were hot! It was a brotherhood of men, and it was easier to suffer the heat and hard work because we suffered together. We were all dirty and sweaty. There seemed to be a pride about how dirty and sweaty we could get.

The men suddenly grew silent. My eyes followed where they were all looking. That's when I first saw her. It was unbelievable.

A beautiful lady was walking into the muddy area in which we were working. She was dressed immaculately. She was wearing a French Waitress outfit in a high collared green jacket with pearls and plunging neckline. She had on a black mini-skirt with black lacy nylon stockings and black high-heeled shoes. She seemed so totally out of place walking in among the workmen.

She carried high on one hand, a silver tray with two long-stemmed crystal glasses filled with something green. In each glass was a small silver spoon.

She walked slowly into a large group of dirty, sweating men and bent over to lower the tray as she delivered one of the glasses to someone there. We couldn't see very well from where we sat on the upside-down buckets. Then she came strutting slowly over to our group next. It really surprised me when she bent over and offered the other glass to me.

It was a glass of frozen mint sherbet.

"My God," I'm thinking, "I can't eat this here in front of these men sitting around me! These are my brothers. They should all have one if I do!"

I got up and walked over to meet the other person who had the other glass of sherbet in the middle of the workplace. It was Father Greg who had come to work as I did, just to help out.

"What is this?" I asked him. "What is this for?"

"I'm not exactly sure what this is all about," he said. "We just have to take these silver spoons and eat this sherbet. There is a political thing going on here, I think."

So we stood there eating the green minty sherbet as the sweating men watched us in silence from all around. Then, after placing the glasses and spoons back on the silver tray where she waited, we went back to our places just in time to hear Lucas say, "OK, men lets get it going again!"

There was a sudden hustle of motion again, and that's how it continued until the sun moved down behind the volcano.

Greg never explained it to me and we never talked about it again. I guess I figured it out by myself soon enough.

"The glasses of sherbet must have come from a rich man in the village," I figured, "who was probably a small benefactor of the school, and who wanted to make sure that no one took ownership of this school who was a poor man, or an unpaid native volunteer worker."

"It was his way of using us to slap them all in the face," I concluded.

Chapter 35

Toasted Peppers

Toasting up my cayenne peppers was one of those household tasks of which one might say, "It's a tough job, but somebody's got to do it."

Every morning at about five-thirty, Monica would put on a pot of water and get it boiling wildly. She liked the flames really whipping up around the sides of the pot.

"Good morning everyone," I'd say as I walked into the big room for breakfast. That was Monica's cue to slide three eggs into the boiling water for four minutes to poach them for my breakfast. Three-minute eggs at our altitude in the mountains took exactly four minutes to do.

"Here are your eggs," she'd say as she rushed them to me at the table, a shaker of ground cayenne pepper in her other hand.

"Thanks, Monica," I'd say, pretending to pick up one of the eggs with my bare hand. She would always forget to bring the silverware.

"Wait! Wait!" she'd say, running to get the silverware and rushing back before I could possibly burn myself.

This was our daily ritual.

If I came into the room as late as seven o'clock, it would be the same ritual. It never changed. If the water wasn't at high boil when I walked into the room, or they ran out of ground cayenne pepper, I think they would mention it in their next confession.

"Water cannot get hotter than 212 degrees," I explained to her. She didn't know what a "degree" was. "Boiling fast did not increase the temperature of water and that simmering would be just fine," I continued, but she didn't know what the word "simmer" meant.

She would not hear of changing the way she did it, so the ritual never changed.

We had built a screened-in wood-fired tortilla kitchen in the back of the house. There the girls would make tortillas and other cooking tasks that needed a grill. One afternoon they called me, "Come and look at something interesting."

"What?" I shouted back at them.

"Come," they said. "You'll see!"

They led me back to the tortilla kitchen and opened the hasp on the screened door and motioned me inside. When I stepped inside the screened area, they stepped back and shut the door and slipped the pin back into the hasp of the door, trapping me inside. They were toasting the cayenne peppers on the grill that they would later grind.

They stood some distance back from the screened-in area, and just watched me trapped inside.

"Hey," I yelled, "let me out of here," The air was thick with the fumes of the toasting peppers and it was burning my eyes and nose and mouth.

"We want you to know what we women have to suffer for your red pepper every morning," they said, laughing and enjoying the tears that were now rolling down my cheeks. "We have to go through this every week for you."

"OK," I said in my commander's voice, "I know now, so let me out." But, that didn't work. I hadn't suffered enough yet.

I tried to begging, humbling myself, and promising things. I acted like it didn't bother me. I even said, "please," but nothing worked.

I think the only reason they released me was because they didn't want the peppers to toast too much. I do know that there was a heightened appreciation for that shaker of ground cayenne pepper every morning.

Chapter 36

The Christmas Innkeeper

What would you answer if Joseph and Mary came asking at your door?

"Knock, knock," it went at our door.

"Yes?" I said looking out of the door. It was a young couple standing there in front of me. The woman was obviously pregnant and they seemed tired of traveling.

"We are looking for a place for the night," said the bearded Joseph. "There is no room at the inn. Can you take us in for the night?"

"No," I answered, to the delight of the candle-bearers and onlookers. "There is no room here for the likes of you!" I added, getting in to their little street drama.

Mary just looked down at the street. Then Joseph said, "Please, we have been traveling all day, and we are tired of searching for a place to stay for the night." Sound familiar?

Well, they actually knocked on my door! ...and I abruptly turned them away!

Can you believe it? Two people dressed up like Joseph and Mary and a small troop of candle-bearers came knocking on the door of our one-room house in the little Guatemalan mountain village in which we lived. Joseph wore a beard and Mary was very pregnant and their story was that they were asking for a place to stay for a few days.

Even the candle-bearers all perked up their ears to hear my answer...

It was all part of a drama. People here often act out stories from the scriptures catching us by surprise in the street at night with their questions. They wanted to understand Joseph and Mary's feelings of continued rejection in their time of need. I quickly sensed their game and fell into the role of the innkeeper who turns them away. I didn't like my part very well, but mine was the door to which they had come.

"No, no, no," I said. "I don't want you here! There just isn't any room for the likes of any of you here!"

And so... with bowed heads by my rejection of them... they slowly and humbly walked away down the street.

...That was their game, and I played out my part of the drama.

I turned them away. And, in the exchange... I learned something about innkeepers.

They acted out this drama to understand the rejection that the real Joseph and Mary must have felt that first Christmas night so long ago. Tonight they walked away in the shoes of Joseph and Mary.

...And me? They didn't know that I experienced something, too. I experienced being selfish and self-centered, while they were learning to understand their own rejection...

But that was only a drama, a dress rehearsal... a preparation for living in real life.

"Working with the poor is a lot like being an innkeeper," I thought. "We innkeepers have to deal with many 'time and space' limitations." It's interesting to be an innkeeper always trying to accommodate the many mountain village families who come to us in their need.

That's how it is when we work for someone for whom there are no limits. There always seems to be time and space for all in God's Inn. It seems that our role in this real life drama is to be here, and keep saying yes.

A few months later there was another drama.

"These things always happen when you least expect it," I said to the two Peace Corps workers who were with me, "and I'm always fair game."

The three of us had been walking through the back streets of a small village, when three or four children approached us.

"We want to ask you something," said one of the children.

"What is it?" asked the young woman of the Peace Corps.

The children looked at each other as if to decide who should speak. Then one of them asked, "Where is Jesus?"

"What?" asked the other Peace Corps worker.

"Where is Jesus?" another child asked. There was no misunderstanding. That is what they asked.

I looked around the village as if to decide where Jesus could be. Then I said, "There he is! He is in that church over there!" I said, pointing and answering their question.

Next the children did something completely unexpected. They reached out their hands as if to give us something. They put a few pennies into our hands. Then they backed up a few yards to watch us.

We were dumfounded. "What is going on here?" the puzzled young lady asked. "Why did these children put pennies in our hands?"

"What day is today?" I asked them.

"Today is Thursday," they both said.

"Yes," I said, "but this is *Holy Thursday*! And we have just played the part of Judas in their little drama!"

We had just betrayed Jesus... and for money!

"So what do we do with this money now?" one of them asked.

"We have to throw the money in the street, just like Judas did," I said, pitching my coins into the street. Then they threw their coins into the street, too. The children were absolutely delighted as they picked up the coins and happily headed down the street again, looking for their next victim.

The next day was Good Friday. We watched the procession and the way they acted out the drama of nailing Jesus to the cross. The ones dressed like Roman soldiers had a hammer and some spikes. As they tried to drive the nails into the hands of the image of Jesus, the women were fighting them as if to prevent them from hurting Jesus.

Finally the fifteen-foot cross is lifted up with Jesus nailed onto it. Everyone dropped to his or her knees and there was an absolute silence.

"Hey, that's mine," a child shouted breaking the silence.

"Throw it again! Harder this time!" was a second shout. There were some children sitting there in the middle of things playing a game with tiny pieces of wax. If you could throw a piece of wax on top of someone else's, and it would stick, you got to keep their piece of wax.

There were maybe a thousand people gathered in that place on their knees, and in complete silence. No one seemed to be bothered much by that noisy intrusion by those few children.

"Why doesn't someone shush them?" I was thinking.

"What on earth are these children thinking? To be sitting under the cross . . . gambling like that!" Then I suddenly realized what was going on . . . They were simply part of the drama.

Chapter 37

Making Chicken Feed

"If we buy the feed we give the chickens, it will be expensive," we decided. "Besides there is another problem…"

"They spray the cotton raised on the coast with too much insecticide," some of the men on the farm had told me, "and we suspect that if cottonseed meal is used as a protein in commercial feed, it's at toxic levels."

"What do you think of making our own feed?" I asked the men sitting around the table who take care of the little farm.

And that's how the feed-making program was born. That's also how I wrote my exhaustive materials list. It was a long list of possible materials that are in abundance that might be used for either feed making or for building materials.

My list had things like banana leaves, chicken bones, the sap from the Australian oak tree, old hard dried-out tortillas, the red coffee bean husks, black beans that were culled out, cornhusks, the cooking water from tortilla making, etc. There were several hundred items on my list.

Not one of these things was used for anything.

"The comfrey tested out at over thirty percent protein," I said. "That's better than alfalfa meal."

"What is this stuff on the table?" asked one of the farm workers, indicating a plastic bag lying on the table full of green powdery material.

"That's comfrey, too," said Jorge, "It's just dried and finely ground. We put it in the feed to raise the protein."

I planted the comfrey in a row like rhubarb plants. It would grow to maturity in about a month, at which time we would saw it off at ground level, chop it up with a machete, dry it, and grind it into a fine green powder. We started with thirty plants, which gave us one plant every day to process.

There were quite a number of very good items on the list that we could collect very cheaply and use in the feed. Some of the children went collecting what we needed to earn a little money.

We got some glass jars in which we placed samples of all the items for which we had found a use so far. These were lined up on several long shelves in our feed workshop with labels indicating their contents.

"I have a bag of chicken bones," said a woman who came. "How much do you pay?"

"We have to weigh them," Pedro would say, "and we pay ten centavos per pound." Then he would weigh them and pay her according to the weight. If we bought commercial bone meal, it would cost five times as much.

People brought their old dry tortillas and we would grind them up. "The analysis says that tortilla meal has the same value as ground corn!" I told them, "besides it has calcium added because of the tortilla making process."

One day I was walking on a back street in a village where most of the streets were dirt streets. The houses were built right up against the street. As I passed by one of the houses, a woman whose house I was walking past, slung a large bowl of warm water out of her door that splashed directly on me and my legs and feet. There I stood surprised to be suddenly soaking wet from the waist down.

"Oh!" she said running out to me, "I'm so sorry! I didn't mean to splash you... You're soaking wet!"

"That's OK," I responded. "I'm sure it was an accident. Don't worry about it." Then I said something really dense. I said, "I was wet when I came into this world, so I've been wet before."

That made her laugh. Then she had to reconstruct the crime to show me what had happened. "I was finishing with rinsing the corn for the tortillas," she began, "and I turned like this... and without looking, I flung the bowl like this..." Unknown to her, there was still some water left in that bowl which came flying at me a second time!

Then we did an instant replay of the last scene.

"What was that stuff in the bowl?" I asked her. It smelled like cooked corn but it was a kind of gooey and slippery liquid.

"That's the corn rinse after I finish cooking the corn." She said, "then I take the corn to the grinder, and that's the dough that tortillas are made from."

"What do you put on the corn when you cook it?" I asked.

"I put calcium and water on about five pounds of corn," she answered. "When it cooks it melts the hard crowns off of the corn so the tortillas turn out softer."

"Then the melted crowns are still in the water when you throw it at other people?" I asked grinning.

"Oh," she joked, "I don't just throw it at anybody. I waited for you to come walking past my house!"

She said I should bring my clothes over later and she would wash them for me. I knew if I just walked away, she would die of guilt. Besides I was getting an idea, so I made another deal with her.

"Next time you have this tortilla water, would you save it for me?" I asked.

"Yes I will," she said. "Come by at this time tomorrow and I'll have it ready. But next time I promise not to throw it at you!"

The next day I took the tortilla water home and boiled it down to a thick paste. Then I spread out the corn paste on a large piece of plastic and let it dry in the sun until it was like a piece of brown flexible leather. I cut up the leathers into strips and ran it through a meat grinder and let it dry some more.

It was really reconstituted corn crowns, but it looked just like brown bits of plastic.

"It has about the same feeding value as regular corn," said the analysis report from the University of North Dakota. They also said that it had higher calcium content than corn and would be ideal for use as chicken feed. They wrote that they didn't know what it was, and would I write and tell them.

"What if we could get all of the tortilla water from the whole village?" I asked my students at the Peace Corps training center near the city. One of them figured it out on a calculator, based on my weight samples and population data.

"It's enough feed ingredient to produce three hundred and sixty-five pounds of chicken every day!" he announced.

That was one little village of twelve thousand people. There are many, many villages pitching a lot of feed value into the streets. Sometimes even at innocent people walking by.

Chapter 38

Witch Doctoring

The idea of doctors treating people in clinics is quite a new thing in most of these mountain villages. Modern medicine is also viewed with suspicion. Many people try to cling to the old ways and often refuse to accept modern medicines.

"Go to see the 'Brucah,' the witch doctor," they tell you. "She will give you some herbs or some tea or something to make you well."

I asked a mother who had an eight-year-old boy who had gotten sick, what she could do for him.

"I will take the leaves from that tree over there," she said, pointing to a rather large tree with dark green leaves, "and I will strip up the leaves and dry them in the sun. Then I will make a thick tea and have him drink it."

"That's got to taste horrible," I commented.

"It's not even that good!" she laughed.

"So how long will it take for him to get well?" I wanted to know.

"He will need to drink some of the tea twice each day for ten days." She answered, "That's all he has to do." She added, "The amoebas will be gone for good."

"Wouldn't it be better to take the two pills for amoebas?" I questioned. "Then he would be feeling great in about three hours, instead of more than a week."

"Not really" was her answer. "If he drinks the tea, the amoebas will not be back for more than a year!" The people in the villages were very conservative, especially about medicine and looking for cures. If the native remedies did not work, they would begin to pray harder. If the person died, they would say that it was God's will.

"Besides," she added, "I don't have to pay anything for those leaves on that tree over there. They're free."

"Go see the Brucah," They told me when I had fallen through the roof of our family center and broke my back. "Only this time," they said, "you will have to go to the Brucah in another village," That meant going through a high and difficult mountain pass.

"They would have to carry me all the way, and then back again," I said. "So I cannot go because the trip would be too difficult in a body cast with a broken back."

"The Brucah in that far village has more power," they said. "She would have you lie on a mat of loosely woven corn stalks that are stretched between four stakes. She would put several small pots with bits of burning charcoal on the earth below you. Then she would put a special mixture of incense in the pots, and the smoke would creep up through the cornstalks and around your body, and drive away the evil."

"She would think that something 'evil' is affecting me?" I asked.

"Probably not," they agreed. "We think the incense is to purify you. She cures you by giving you something you must drink, and then she rattles a bunch of chicken-bones in patterns around you while she chants something."

"The cure only takes about an hour," said one of the group.

Once when I had cut into the side of my hand with a machete. I went to see the local witch doctor or "Brucah" who only lives about fifty yards down the street from where we live. She has jars and pots of stuff setting all over her house, as well as a lot of plants growing in hanging baskets everywhere.

"What can you do for this?" I asked holding out my hand.

"Come in and I will try something," she said leading me into her house where I had to dodge a couple of pots a little too low for my height. She laughed at my difficulty moving about in her low-roofed house.

"I don't think you were expecting me," I said referring to the low-hanging potted plants.

We sat down at the table, and she mixed some things together and began spreading it on my wound. It was like a fine reddish mud. "Now I'm really going to get infected," I thought.

She pressed part of a plant leaf into the mud and tied it with three cornhusk strips. "Keep it away from water for three days," she instructed me when she had finished. It actually worked quite well and left no scar. It was a little awkward going around with those cornhusks tied on and avoiding water on my hand for three days.

About two months later, in the middle of the night, this same Brucah woman was knocking on my door. "What is it?" I asked, with the most wide-awake face I could make.

"My daughter has a very high fever and I can't bring it down," she said excitedly. "Come! We must take her to the doctor at the clinic right now!"

"I will bring the jeep," I said quickly. Off she ran to her house down the street. I quickly put on my shoes and clothes and drove to her house nearby. When I got there the mother was helping the fourteen-year-old daughter towards the jeep.

"Get in the back seat first," I told the mother, but she tried to crawl in with her arms only, and leaving her feet outside. It took awhile, but she finally got in with me placing her last foot inside the door. Then I got the daughter seated on the front seat, put the blanket around her, and closed the jeep door.

When I got around into the drivers seat, I could see that there was still a problem with the mother. She was on her knees on the floor, facing backwards looking out of the back window of the jeep. "She doesn't know which way this thing goes," I thought.

"She has never ridden in a vehicle before!" I suddenly realized. It took awhile, but I finally got her to sit on the seat facing forwards rather than kneeling backwards. Then we began driving through the streets.

The doctor lived a mile away diagonally through the village. We would be making lots of right and left turns to get there. We had to make a left turn in the next intersection. Both of my riders fell against the right side of the jeep because they didn't know to brace themselves and they couldn't see anything in the darkness of the night.

"You've got to hang on somewhere," I said to the mother riding in the back. I quickly took hold of the girl's shoulder with my right hand to steady her on the many turns we had to make before we got there. Except for moments when I had to shift, I drove with only my left hand.

We got the girl into a bed in the clinic and the doctor gave her a shot of penicillin. "Keep her covered," I said to the mother as I left. The next morning I found out that this young woman had pneumonia. Her fever left her the next day and a few days later she went home.

The house-girls loved my story the next morning about getting them in the car and all. They liked the idea of the Brucah coming for medicine when things got really difficult

"Weren't you afraid to drive the jeep through the streets with just your left hand?" they asked.

"No, why should I be?" I asked. "After all, God created the whole world with just his left hand."

"He did?" they asked looking at each other. "Why didn't he use both hands?"

"Because," I answered laughing, "Jesus was sitting on his right hand."

Chapter 39

The Working Mothers

One day a woman came to the project house with four children.

"Hi," I said. "How can I help you?" She did not answer, and it seemed like she did not know what she wanted or how we could help. "So… what is your name?" I asked.

"Maria," she answered slowly. She was holding her little baby girl, and her three boys were surrounding her and hanging on to her. They were actually hanging on and milling around her at the same time.

"And what is your name?" I asked the oldest boy who was clinging on to her dress.

"My name is Jorge," said the boy looking up at his mother, as if to ask her if he got his name right.

"And your brother, what is his name?" I asked, indicating one of them.

"Miguel," came the answer. I just pointed, indicating the last one, and he said, "My little brother is Tono."

Maria seemed to have an anxious and worried look. I looked at her little girl and asked her name, and how old she was.

"Her name is Cindy," she answered, "and she will be one year old next week."

Most people know what they want when they come to our door. This woman wasn't sure what to say… We went and sat down in some chairs nearby and talked. She told me how her husband was killed in a bus accident six months ago, and now she was alone with these children.

In our conversation I learned that she was washing clothes at the public clothes-washing tank in her tiny village, when she heard some of the other women talking about our project and what we do. They gave her our address, but when she tried to find us she got lost because she didn't know how to read the directions. She couldn't read the street signs either, and ended up having to return to her home again.

"So how did you find us now?" I asked.

"I waited until one of the other women I met, needed to come here, and I followed them," she answered, "but it was hard to keep up with all of these children going with me and slowing me down." Later I learned that she walked, following the other woman some three or four miles to get to our door.

By now her three boys sat in every one of the dozen chairs at least three or four times each. Suddenly they began lining up the chairs to make a train or something.

"What do you do here?" Maria asked quietly with an air of nervousness. Then I realized that she didn't have a clue as to what we could do for her. She overheard the other women talking and saying how we've helped them, and so she came.

"We help women who are widows and who have three or four children to support," I said enjoying her growing smile. I had just received fifty dollars that my bishop sent me, and I was getting an idea of where to spend it for him.

"Use it where it's most needed," he wrote.

"Get into the jeep," I told them, not knowing that these children had never been in a vehicle before. They had a fun ride back to their house.

"This is where we live," said Maria. It was a very small wooden house with a cement floor. It was kind of messed up, but livable. She could wash her clothes about a block away at the public cement washing tank. There was a kitchen outside, but there was no firewood.

"Are you renting this room?" I asked.

"Yes, I have to pay rent, but I'm only two months behind on paying it," she confessed. "I'm trying to catch up... I'm working every day as much as I can. I have to go up the mountain and search for firewood every day, too."

Then, while wiping the tears, she told me how every morning she fed those children whatever food she had. Then she would lock them in the little one-room house, while she went out looking for work. She would go up and down the streets of the larger village nearby, and beg for people to let her wash their clothes and iron them. Then she would go knocking at doors again looking for another person who would hire her to wash their clothes.

At the end of the day she would go home. She said she was always worried and a little afraid to open the door because her children were alone all day. The oldest is only seven and that's too young to take care of the other three. "Sometimes they were really dirty and crying when I got there."

"Do you know what a day-care is?" I asked her. She shook her head negatively. "It's a place like a school that takes care of small children while their mothers go to work," I told her, "and I know a good day-care that is run by the state, so it's free of cost."

"Get into the jeep," I said. "I'll take you there!" They liked riding in the jeep, I think. The children's day-care place was about two miles distance from their house. It was a happy place where there were lots of children and they had lots of young women who took care of them. Her children could begin coming there right away.

There are drivers in the area who make a business of picking up and delivering children to their schools every morning and later in the day when school is out, they drive them home again. "This we will have to pay for," I told her. "We will make arrangements with a driver who drives out to your village."

"In order for you to get your kids ready for day-care or off to school, you will need a watch and learn to tell time. That way you will know when to expect them home again, too, I explained.

"These are things that I didn't know about," said Maria, who seemed to be seeing a world of which she knew nothing.

"Maybe we can find a permanent job for you, too, Maria," I suggested, "so you can earn a better wage, and maybe go to classes where you can learn to read and write and do numbers."

Their world was made of dreams for today, but tomorrow would begin a new world of reality for them. They knew that Miguel would soon be enrolled in the first grade of a very good school, and that there would be sponsoring godparents for all of them eventually.

I told them to pray for a good bishop tonight who was willing to help them, even when he didn't even know them. And then I left that woman holding little Cindy in her arms, and with her three boys still buzzing around her.

When Maria came into the project house a few days later, I was in the midst of dealing with an identical problem with two other widows who didn't know how to read or write either, and who were trying to support themselves and their children by washing and ironing clothing for others, too, just as Maria was doing.

"We must live 'hand to mouth' from hour to hour," they were telling me. "Every day we are in a crisis to keep the children healthy and fed. There are many of us who are abandoned or widowed, so there is too much competition for the menial work available."

"The little money we have does not go far enough," said Maria, "and people always take advantage of us."

"How do they take advantage of you?" I asked them.

One of the women named Juana answered, "In the market they find out that we don't understand numbers, so they charge too much and give us the wrong change."

"When you buy potatoes," I asked the group, "is it cheaper to get five for a dollar, or pay a quarter for each?" Not one of the three women knew which was a better deal. "Is it better to get six small potatoes, or four big ones?" Most of them thought it was better to get six because six is more than four.

All of these women were way behind on their rent, and had

almost no available money for food. So, I got an idea. They needed food for their families, and I needed some information. They could help me get my information, and at the same time get some food for their families.

"You three women can work for me today, and you will earn some food for your families," I began.

"What do we have to do," asked Juana.

"I am going to have each of you go to the open market and buy forty dollars worth of food as though you were shopping for your family," I explained. "You must spend all of the forty dollars, and you must bring all of the food back here to the project house so I can see what each of you has purchased."

"We're going to the open market to buy food?" asked Maria.

"Yes," I continued, "and I want you to try to remember all of the prices you pay for everything, if you can."

"After you get back here, we will weigh your foods and we will make a complete list of the items and their weights and prices," I said. "After that you can each have all of the food you have purchased to take home with you. So buy things as wisely as you can."

"So we get to keep all we have bought?" asked the third woman, who thought this was too good to be true.

"Yes," I said. "The food you buy will be your pay for working for me today." Then off they went to the market. Each of them had a son or daughter to help carry things and remember the prices paid for everything.

The results were very revealing. The sellers at the market cheated them badly. They bought items with greatly varying prices. They chose many items that were not very good nutritional foods. Many of the items were not even food items at all.

The data that I received was very helpful for me in understanding what elements these disadvantaged women needed to learn about shopping. These women provided me with the very information I needed to help them. Now I knew how to teach them what they needed to know.

They were the ones who gave me the answers to their own problems.

Chapter 40

Farm Wedding

"What a great road for four-wheeling!" I said to Father John as we bounced along the back mountain roads in the red Toyota truck. "So… we're going to a wedding." I said.

"Yes, we are." He repeated, "We are going to a wedding! And you should find this interesting. Did you bring your camera?" he asked, knowing I'm a wedding photographer.

"Yes, I did," I responded. We stopped talking for a minute to hold on better as we bounced through a very rough spot.

All of the people who lived in the rows of houses on this particular farm would be there. There was a school, a church, a small store, and about sixty or eighty families. The school only had the first three grades. If someone wanted to study more than three years, they would have to go elsewhere.

There were a lot of people walking around as we drove into the housing area and up near the church.

"Shooting a wedding here is going to be fun for me." I thought, as I pulled the camera from my backpack and put the strap around my neck. "Things wouldn't get going for another fifteen minutes or so," I thought, as I walked around and scoped out the area.

"What a nice day for a wedding," I said, to a small group of people gathering near the church. "My name is David, and I came with Father John," I said, shaking everyone's hand. "It's very nice to meet all of you."

They told me their names and we talked for a while. "Where are you from?" one of them asked.

"I'm from the States," I answered. "I live near where Father John comes from." After ten minutes, there was a sudden movement towards the church and people began to slowly enter the church to get a place to sit.

I was surprised to see the bride coming up the pathway on

her way to the church. She was walking with two of her friends as if they were only walking to school. The bride was very young, and I knew that she was the bride because she was wearing a white veil. Her dress was nice, but an ordinary dress that was simple and appropriate. I took a couple of photographs of them walking together before they noticed me.

"By the church gate," I said pointing to the white gate. I took a picture. "Arm in arm together," I said and took another. "Don't laugh," I said, and I took another picture of them laughing.

There was a line of people waiting in a slow moving line going into the small church. The three girls got into the line and, to my amazement, entered the church when their turn came. "My," I thought to myself. "What humility for the bride to enter the church in line with everyone else."

Most of the people were dressed in their best ordinary clothes. I wasn't able to pick out the one who was the groom yet. The bride sat with her family near the front. And soon the ceremony began. Father John made some remarks, introduced the bride and groom, and began with the first readings…

"The groom was very young," I thought. His shirt was a little large and his black pants were a little short. "He probably borrowed the shirt from his stout friend, and the pants from his shorter brother," I figured.

Even with the microphone, no one heard their vows or saw much of their faces. It actually happened pretty fast amid nervousness and tears. I have a wonderful picture of them during that formal solemn moment. Then there was a moment of question as they counted out the thirteen coins. One of them gave the coins to the other as a traditional symbol. Then they sat together on a small bench placed to one side until the ceremony was over. I think they were relieved to be out of the spotlight.

The reception and dinner was in a large room where they usually stacked sacks of freshly picked coffee during picking time. They had many chairs, but only a few tables for serving the dinner.

"Come with me," said a well-dressed gentleman, as he led me to the center table. "Please sit here," he said smiling, and he indicated a chair. "So, you're from Minnesota," he began, and sat down beside me.

"Yes," I said, "I haven't been here in your country long. I enjoy your wedding customs, too. They seem like a very nice couple."

"I agree," he said. At that moment someone came and asked him something and he gave some instruction to them. "I agree," he repeated turning back to me. "That young man has worked for me here on our farm since he finished his schooling."

He was the farm owner. We barely finished the introductions around the table, when the plates of food came.

Father John, who was on the other side of the table, prompted the farm owner to say the prayer, and he did well. Then we began the wedding meal. The farm owner's wife and one of his sons were there, the parents of the groom, the owner's mother and grandson.

"The bride and groom are not seated at a table," I thought to myself. "This is really strange." So I looked around and finally saw the two of them sitting with the other people also waiting to eat. The bridal couple was seated on two little stools that were too low for them. They were not talking. They were just sitting there against the wall, with their knees sticking up too high, looking very bored.

"The bride and groom are not seated at a table," I mentioned to the owner, thinking that they had been forgotten.

"Oh," he said smiling, "They have to wait and will probably get seated at this table when we finish." Later I took their picture. I have a great picture of them sitting on those two low stools waiting and bored.

I imagined that the groom would be at his farm work the next day, and she would be up early making tortillas for him. And that would be their life together in house number forty-three or something forever and ever.

They didn't get to sit at the table when we left because it wasn't their turn yet. So I stole them away with me back to the church. We lit candles and took pictures, we put flowers together and took pictures, and we gathered some of their friends and took pictures.

We took pictures at their house, which turned out to be number twenty-six. We stopped at the bridge and they walked towards me hand in hand. We did some close-ups near some bright red flowering vines hanging over a wall.

Then I rushed them back to the coffee shed and, handed them over to their parents, taking one final shot of them with parents and farm owners.

"I'm ready," I said to Father John, who was with some people near the red Toyota truck. Soon we were heading back up the mountain. I printed maybe twenty or twenty-five enlarged color photographs, which I placed in a leather album and delivered to them a month later.

They may have to work hard, and live humbly, and stay in such lowly circumstances for the rest of their lives. But at least they'll have the most envied wedding album on the entire mountainside.

Chapter 41

The Peanut Girl

"Buy some peanuts today!" said nine-year-old Juana, with a bit of anxiousness in her voice. "Look at these peanuts . . . These are the best peanuts . . . You must buy!" she continued, holding the basket in front of my face.

I shouldn't have looked at them!

"No, go away! I don't want any peanuts today," I said with finality. It didn't make any difference what I said now. She had caught me looking at her lousy peanuts in her stupid basket... Now she had a delighted expression on her face! She saw me look at her peanuts. Now it was too late.

"No! No! No!" I repeated in a raised voice. That's a mistake, too. A raised voice only means that you want to buy peanuts, but at a lower price. All that's left is the haggling over price. . . . And she never loses that battle.

'Yes! Yes!" she said. At that she sat down and began to weigh out some peanuts in her balance scale. "How many pounds was it that you said you wanted? Did you say one pound or two pounds?"

"I am not going to buy any peanuts today!" I said, "I don't even like peanuts. They make me sick when I eat them!"

"So you do eat them!" she said laughing. "Here," she continued, "I'm going to give you a free peanut as a sample." She took out a peanut and put it into my hand.

"Is this one really free?" I asked her. "I don't have to buy anything if I eat it?"

"It's free," she said. At that I cracked open the peanut and ate it. Then I turned and tried to walk away from her.

She was running beside me now, easily keeping up. "Now you have to buy!" She said loudly, "because now you owe me because you ate my sample. Hey, you owe me!"

"OK," I said, "How much for your one silly peanut?"

"Ten cents," she said. "After all I have to go through to lose that one peanut, that's cheap."

"So how much for a pound?" I heard myself asking... "What am I doing? Why do I need to know how much per pound, when I'm not buying any peanuts? What am I thinking?"

"Sixty cents for a pound," she said.

"I'll give you forty," I said. "Take it or leave it."

"I have to pay fifty cents a pound when I buy them!" she said. "How can I sell them to you for less than I pay for them?"

"OK, I'll give you forty-five cents," I offered.

"No, fifty-five cents and no lower." Juana answered.

"Then we have no deal!" I said finally. "Go sell your peanuts to a rich person. See that man over there?" I asked,

"There?" she asked pointing to a man on the street.

"Yeah, that one," I said. "He loves peanuts. He is waiting for you to sell to him. He is very rich." And off I walk again, a little faster this time.

'OK," she yells running after me, "fifty cents." And she sits down to weigh out a pound of peanuts with her scale. She looked up and said, "I knew you liked peanuts!" and goes on with her weighing. Finally she dumps them into a plastic bag and gets ready to tie the bag. Before she does, she deliberately takes one peanut out of my plastic bag and throws it back into her basket.

"So, what's that for? That's my peanut! Put that peanut back in my plastic bag!" I demanded.

"Too late," she said. "I've already tied the bag."

I watch her walk away down the street feeling very satisfied with herself. "She is going to look for another victim now!" I figured.

I'm not sure if she charmed me with her smile, or it was those large dancing brown eyes and positive attitude that finally got to me. It certainly wasn't the peanuts. She uses a lot of that charm when she sells peanuts to passersby. Her nine years have taught her more than some of us ever learn.

Once I took two bags of her peanuts home and set them on my desk beside my electronic postage scale. Then I got an idea. I would weigh these two bags of her peanuts and check out her little balance scale.

"She is going to have to fix her little balance scale weights," I thought. "There are only eleven ounces in each bag."

Next time I bought peanuts from her, which was the next time she came along, I waited until she had finished weighing out my bag of peanuts.

Then I said to her, "I'm going to take this bag of peanuts home and weigh it on my little scale. If it weighs less than a pound, I will never, never buy peanuts from you again... as long as I live!"

She calmly reached into her basket, grabbed as many peanuts as she could with both hands, and dumped them into the plastic bag she was getting ready for me, and said, "I wasn't finished!"

I think I won that battle, but I may have lost the war!

Nothing is as exasperating as having clever children around like that who know more than I do. She usually stays one or two steps ahead of everyone. It took months for us to figure out how she could make anything selling peanuts for the same price she paid for them.

That's when I tried to get her into school. You see, she thinks there are only eleven ounces in a pound. So... every once in awhile we end up with some children who are educating us . . .

. . . instead of the other way around.

Chapter 42

The Train Cars

"Now that could get boring…" I thought to myself, "to be cranking out school desks day after day in the carpentry shop. The men need a change of pace."

"We can never sacrifice the quality for speed," was our motto. That's why we took fifteen minutes every day about mid-morning to do a quality control session… discussing the work, exploring new ideas from the men, and figuring out better ways to do things.

That really streamlined the workflow and gave the men ownership to the work they did. Every once in awhile, though, the workers needed a break from the regular day after day desk-building.

"We are going to build some little wooden trucks," I told the men one day, holding up a prototype model. "We will use this model as a guide in building them."

"How are we going to make the wheels?" one of them asked.

"We will use the turning lathe," I answered. "We will make a long round roller, then saw the wheels off with one of the radial arm saws. Making the axles will be a problem. Some of you can start figuring out a way to do that."

"Why not use a pencil?" suggested another man.

"Because the final test of these trucks is that we have to be able to pull it rolling along the floor… with a full grown man standing on it with all of his weight!"

They went to work with a new enthusiasm. They could use their creativity. Soon they had several models to consider. The first one we examined was way too large. It looked pretty much like the model but it took two men to lift it.

Another one had very wobbly wheels that kept falling off, but it looked pretty good. "We don't think this will support the weight of a man standing on it," they volunteered.

The third model was interesting. "This one looks very strong and rolls very well," I began, "and it's about the right size and has a very fine finish." They were very proud of this one.

"It does have one little problem," I said cautiously. "On this other side there is a very large gaping crack in the wood." The main part of the truck had an unforgiving inch-wide open crack in the wood.

"You have to look at the truck," they explained, "from this other side. Come over here and look at it. It looks great."

"If a family were to buy this truck in a U.S. store and it had this crack," I reasoned with them, "they would take it back and get their money back."

"Any child on the street," they argued, "would love to have this little truck to play with. What kind of children have to have a perfect truck anyway?"

That was the hardest part of my work at the little factory. I had to teach them to make things that were perfect. "Can't they see a gaping crack on one side? Or a gash across one of the wheels? Or saw marks along the body of the truck?" I wondered. "Can you see this truck top that is sawed crooked?" I asked the group one day, during the first months of operation.

"Maybe it's alright to be a little crooked," volunteered one of them. At that moment, my eye caught a glimpse of one worker who was sitting with his feet propped up on a pile of scrap lumber. He was wearing two left shoes. That's when I figured it out! There was a logical answer.

Not one thing in their lives was perfect! Their streets were crooked and had rocks sticking out everywhere. Their fences were not straight. Every pathway in this village twisted and curved. Their clothes were full of patches. Even their houses were not square. Every tin roof in this village dipped in one direction or the other. And their shoes...

Eventually the little wooden trucks were perfect!

The men built boxes and boxes of beautiful twenty-inch wooden semi-trucks that were exported to the States.

They were exact copies of my original prototype but made from a beautiful variety of woods. These trucks had a finer finish that felt good to the touch. The wood grains were beautiful and they were perfect.

Another year passed by quickly. The factory produced many more school desks for the increasing number of classrooms we were building in the next village. Then it became time for another divergence in the work.

"This is a little wooden toy train," I said, holding up the little train cars that a carpenter in the States built for a prototype. "We're going to try to build little wooden trains like this for the toy market," I added.

"Study these models, and try to make exact copies," I instructed them. "See who can make the best copy!" I added to challenge them. There was an engine, coal car, tanker, log car, boxcar, and a caboose.

I placed the train on a table in an open space in the middle of the shop. "Study the model cars," I said, "Then measure, plan, saw, sand, build, and finish cars of your own." The dozen men and four or five work-study students went right to work with a new enthusiasm.

Every December we took a break from regular work, too. I gave the workers three weeks of paid time to build furniture or toys for their families. There was a limit on the square feet of lumber they could use for free. There would be a contest and we'd put their work on display and give a prize to the best item at our Christmas dinner party. One of them made a complete train for his kids.

"Why don't you put the train in the right order?" I asked them one day, noticing that the cars were out of order on the display table. In fact, the cars were always out of order… and I kept arranging them correctly.

"What should the order be?" asked one of the men.

"Well," I began, "this is the engine car, and this is the caboose, and this is the coal car . . ."

"What's a caboose?" came the next question, "and what's a coal car?"

"A caboose is the train office," I explained, "and the coal car has to follow the engine."

"So… where does the engine go?" another asked.

"These are awfully funny questions," I thought to myself. "They all had straight faces, so they weren't joking. So, what was it?"

"How many of you have ever seen a train?" I asked. They just sat there and looked at each other. "No one?" No one had ever seen a train. Then I remembered something about our location…

We were in a village on a mile high mountainside for cripe sakes! They had never seen a train! What was I thinking?

Chapter 43

Bean Inoculation

Many people of the mountain villages consider themselves to be farmers. Early in the morning they begin the climb upwards on the volcano to their cornfields and bean fields. They planted on the sides of the slopes at tremendous angles. It was so steep that they often tied themselves to a tree stump or something as they worked, so they wouldn't misstep and literally fall out of their cornfield and hurt themselves.

"You have to work very hard for a very low yielding harvest," I told the men gathered for my corn school. "Is there any way that you could fertilize your corn," I asked the group.

"We can't carry commercial fertilizer up there," said one of the men, "It's too heavy and too steep a climb with sacks of fertilizer."

"Most of us can't afford to buy fertilizer," offered another. "We don't have much money. We could buy enough fertilizer to use on some of the lower fields. All of us have land on the lower plain."

"There is a way that we can fertilize the upper fields," I stated to the group, "without buying fertilizer and without carrying anything up there." They looked mystified by my impossible statement.

"How can we do that?" was the general consensus.

"I tested your soil to see what it lacks," I said. "Who remembers what it lacks?" Almost all of them remembered that "nitrogen" was what it lacked. "You grow corn, and then plant beans beside the corn so the beans can climb up the cornstalks, right?" I asked.

"Yes," one of them said, "but how does that get more nitrogen into the soil?"

"There is something that you can put on the bean seed when you plant the beans," I explained. "It makes the bean's leaves take nitrogen out of the air, and their roots put the nitrogen into the soil." They looked at each other as if to question this whole story of mine. "It's as simple as that." I concluded.

"It's called 'inoculation' of the seed," I said, "and without inoculating the bean seed, it doesn't happen."

"Where do we get this stuff to inoculate our bean seed," they all seemed to be asking.

"Oh," I said with a grin, "I have a fifty-pound bag of it in my jeep! I brought three bags of it with me in the airplane from the States. For our class today, we need less than a pound."

We carried all of the stuff we needed to a flat place on the edge of a nearby cornfield that belonged to one of the men.

"First we need a little bit of milk," I said holding up a pint jar of milk. "I got this bottle of goat's milk this morning. Anyone thirsty?" No one was thirsty.

I then spread out about a square yard of plastic on the ground, poured about a pound of bean seed on the plastic, and slopped some of the milk on the beans enough to make them wet. Next I reached into my bag of inoculant, which was a black powder, and put a small handful of it on the beans.

"Mixing it is the most fun," I said to break the silence. Then I mixed it with a few stirs of the muddy looking beans, and began to spread out the beans over the entire piece of plastic. "It's important that they dry well," I said. "So leave them alone until they are good and dry."

"Now it's your turn," I said to the group, as I began handing out the plastic sheets I had cut. "Remember," I added, "don't use too much milk or too much inoculant." They each found a good spot on the ground and did their mixing and spreading just the way that I had.

Then we went to some of the half-grown corn nearby and I showed them how to plant the seed without rubbing off too much of the black inoculant coating on the bean seed.

"Now these bean plants," I reminded them, as we washed up in the nearby stream, "will work for you by taking the nitrogen out of the air and putting it into the soil. This will save you work, money, and increase your corn crop."

"How many of you will do this when you plant your beans?

Instead of a large showing of hands, there wasn't one hand up. This meant that they wouldn't do it. "Aren't you going to do it?" I asked surprised.

Each of them shook their head, "no," in turn as I looked at them.

"But why not?" I asked, not understanding, "There are so many advantages! I'm giving you all of the inoculant you'll need…"

Then one of them looked up at me, hesitated, and then said, "We're afraid that if we use this stuff on our seed, our children will die."

"Why will your children die?" I asked.

"They will be poisoned," he said, "because that black stuff is the same stuff we use to kill rats… That stuff is poison!" he said. I could see that they all agreed with him. Their rat poison must look like the inoculant!

"If this is poison," I said as I grabbed a three-finger bunch of the inoculant out of the bag, "then I'll say 'goodbye' to all of you now." I then put the inoculant into my mouth and ate it, swallowing it down. They looked very alarmed.

"Hey, this is good!" I said reaching for more and eating another bunch of it. I have often wondered if it was more interesting for me to watch them, or for them to watch me. Then I offered the bag to them to have some, too, as though it were a bag of cookies.

They told me months later that they got a bumper crop.

Chapter 44

Loading the Bus

"The luggage racks up on top of the village busses are not only for baskets and sacks of things, pails, barrels, crates of chickens, items tied up in large nettings, and dilapidated boxes without end, beat-up and worn with their flaps blowing in the wind…" we explained.

"People often ride up there, too, when the inside of the bus down below is filled," we said to our visitors.

"But, how can anybody…" they began in wonderment.

"It's important to get to where you are going," we said, "at any cost. They just have to hang on tight, when riding on top, or they will get a shorter ride than they expected." The busses look like school busses on first look. They all have caterpillar engines, though, for climbing the steep mountain grades, and racks on top and ladders on the back for carrying things up there.

"How many people fit in a bus?" is often the question, "and 'ten more' is most often the answer."

"They fill up the seats first, then someone gets to sit on the lap of each seated person." We explained further, "but the bus is only considered half full at that point. There is still space for a large number of people who can pack themselves in standing positions in the center aisle all the way to the front, right down to the doorway.

The drivers love to roar around the mountain curves with their powerful engines cranked, sometimes with a child on their lap for whom they are baby-sitting. They often have a picture of John Paul II hanging up front and that, along with a rosary dangling somewhere is protection enough.

Boarding one of these busses in the city is a wilder experience than riding.

"The bus will come soon," said Max. "How much stuff do you have?" he asked.

"Well," I said looking at our stuff, "we've got two sacks of concentrate, this large bag of stuff, and this box of baby chickens that have to ride inside."

Max was a fellow we knew from one of our villages about four hours away. It was the village where we were headed, too.

"There are a lot of people here waiting for this bus," I said to him, looking around at the crowd of people. "We won't all fit on the bus, I'm sure."

"Don't worry, I'll help get you on the bus alright," he said confidently.

Suddenly the bus was driving up towards us! Every one grabbed their baskets and boxes and ran towards the bus as fast as they could. I was afraid somebody would get run over. It was amazing. Every one was running in competition for a seat or place in the bus, and suddenly every one was every one else's enemy.

...Every one except Max who had promised to help us.

He was walking casually and relaxed with us towards the bus. There was a sea of people in front of us, crowding around, all pushing and trying to get into the door of the bus at the same time. There was a moment when suddenly the door of the bus opened...

"Follow me," said Max running at the crowd and leaping forward and floating headfirst over the top of everyone and some-how landing and getting into the door first! As people split in his wake for a second, we were suddenly able to move directly to the door, too and went into the bus taking our seat while the bus was still empty.

"I'll be back!" he said and out the back door he went, slid-ing over the top of the crowding people trying to enter through the back door, and disappearing somewhere outside. He was taking care of our sacks and other things, getting them up on top of the bus where the luggage goes. There was a constant pushing and shouting around us on the inside as the bus filled up with people. I heard a rapping on the window and there was Max with our for-gotten box of chickens, ready to slide them inside through the window.

We felt the bus begin to grind forward an inch or two. Then we felt vibrations as the driver gunned the engine and bit-by-bit moved the bus forward maybe a foot or so.

"This is a crazy business," I said as we put the box of chicks in the only available space remaining on the inside luggage rack. It took only minutes... maybe seconds to load up that bus. Suddenly there was almost no one left outside. We had been trying to save a seat for Max, but he didn't return and the pressure of people had encroached on any possible space in the seat that we were scrunched in.

Suddenly I saw him. Max was sitting across the aisle in a window seat as if by magic, waving to us as if to ask, "Is there anything else I can get you?"

There was an intimacy about being packed in so tight with the people around us. Except for the pig sitting on the man's lap in the seat ahead of us, and the half grown chickens running around the floor that a small girl was trying desperately to catch and put back in her basket, it seemed that we were part of this strange culture that seemed less foreign... at least for the moment.

Chapter 45

The Sprinkling Can

I got to know a man who took care of a large vegetable garden near the house where we lived. He would grow almost every kind of vegetable you could imagine.

I often gave him new seeds so he could try out new varieties of vegetables.

Day after day he was there watering or planting or hoeing. On market days he was out there when the rooster was still crowing, filling baskets with the things he wanted to sell. Then we'd see him trudging past the house on his way to the market with his loaded wheelbarrow to make his sales.

It was difficult learning his name. The first time I asked him, he said his name was: "Miguel Antonio Pablo Agusto Diego Juan Lopez Gonzalez." He rattled off his complete list of six baptismal names so fast I didn't get it. Then he repeated them even faster, and I heard some names but didn't know which of the names I should use, so I just thought of him as Mr. McGreggor, because he had trouble with rabbits in his garden. His name turned out to be "Pablo."

"Your water hose leaks pretty bad, Pablo," I said to him one day across the fence.

He used the "French Intensive" method of gardening that was popular. That means the plants grow on a flat raised area one meter by three meters, and the pathways are narrow between them. They called these rectangular areas "tables" because they were about the size of a table, I suppose.

"Yeah," he said, "the pathways flood with water and I have to wear those rubbers on my shoes" His hose was really a disaster. It had tiny holes that caused it to spray shoots of little showers out about four or five feet in half a dozen places.

"I think I could fix that for you," I told him.

"How do you fix a leaky old hose like that?" he asked.

"Oh," I said, thinking about the tubes of JB Weld epoxy glue I had in my toolbox. "I have some 'stuff' that can fix it so it won't leak anymore." He became curious. "After I fix it, though, you can't use the hose for the rest of that day," I continued.

"When can you do this?" he asked.

"I'll do it when you are done with the hose for the day," I replied. We decided in about two hours would be a good time.

He sat and watched intently as I opened my toolbox and took out the two tubes of epoxy glue, a piece of old rag, and a knife. I also had some three-inch lengths of half inch black plastic pipe that fit inside his hose.

I picked up the hose at its first leaky spot. Then I took my sharp Swiss Army knife in my other hand and got ready to cut the hose in half. I glanced up at him just before I cut the hose off...

"I've got to stop him," he must have been thinking. His face was scrunched up like it was going to hurt.

I quickly sliced off the hose. I cut it in six more places where there were little holes. It was now in many pieces. He seemed to be suffering a little over losing his only hose that he must have had since the dawn of creation.

"How do you like your hose now?" I teased. The poor man just shook his head.

He watched intently as I mixed the magic tubes of 'stuff' together on a small piece of cardboard with a nail. Then I buttered up the little pieces of black plastic pipes, and pushed them between the places where I had cut the hose, splicing them back together again, putting his entire precious hose back into one piece again.

"That's it!" I said. "Just leave the hose lay there until tomorrow morning, and you can begin using it again then." When I left him, he was standing there looking at his hose that had died and was now resurrected.

"It's like a new one!" he said excitedly the next day. "And the pathways are dry," he added. "The connection still leaks there where it screws onto the faucet," he said indicating the water squirting out.

I walked back to my toolbox, got a rubber hose washer, put it in the connection and the squirting stopped.

"See the tiny hole in the bottom of my sprinkling can, where the water sprays on my shoe when I carry it," he said to me next day when he brought his sprinkling can over to the fence to show me. I mixed up more epoxy.

Later that week as I walked past his garden, he motioned me inside to show me something. It was the sprinkler head of the sprinkling can this time. "See my pant leg?" he said, "it always gets wet because it sprays a little stream of water sideways when I sprinkle the vegetables."

When I handed the fixed sprinkling can back to him, he was pointing towards the handle.

"What's wrong with the handle, Pablo?" I ask very curious, because the handle can't leak.

"Well," he explained, "the handle is a *flat* handle, and my hand would fit better if the handle were *more round*." I suddenly realized that I had finished this job and it was time for me to go now.

"What are you going to do about that handle?" I heard him ask. But, I just smiled and shook his hand and wished him well, before leaving.

Chapter 46

Angela's Joy

Today, in one of our villages, I wired up a house we had built for a family who had been reduced to living on the street when we found them. Everybody helped out.

It's fun to watch the children when we finally turn on the electrical power. "Carmen, stop flipping that switch on and off like that!" said her father, after we turned the power on. Each of the children seemed to want to flip the light switch ten or twenty times and marvel at the light going off and on. It's probably like a magic show for them. They have never lived where there were electric lights before.

I remember the "family building crew" we employed when we hauled the materials out to the place where we built their house. Even the kids found wonderful ways to be helpful.

We first loaded the lumber and sheet steel and nails and things in our pickup truck and hauled them out to the location where the family members and our handful of volunteers were going to build the house.

"Stack everything straight in the truck!" we kept saying, "Don't put the lumber in every which way." There was a tendency to disorganize. We actually had to unload the corrugated steel roofing, and then reload it in a straight pile so it wouldn't get bent up.

Laying out the house so it was square and level were new concepts in this neighborhood. "These volunteers are extremely exacting and demanding," they must have thought, "to use a tape measure, a square, and a level… instead of guesswork and eye-balling things."

The children helped by handing me things like switches and screws and tools and black electrical tape. "Place the nails like this so the wood will not split," I say to the family helpers, "and hold the hammer with your hand back farther on the handle so the nails won't bend over." This was the first experience for our helpers.

Members of this family have never held a hammer in their hand before, so there was quite a lot of teaching and learning taking place.

"A screw turns the other way around to tighten it, William," I explain to my ten-year-old helper. Then I handed him a tape measure and asked him to mark and saw a two-foot piece off of a board. "This is how you extend the tape," I said as I showed him. He had never measured anything before. I tried to show him how to measure but he couldn't read numbers because he had never been to school. We sat down and I taught him the number symbols and what he needed to know about numbers and feet and inches before we could go on.

It seems to me that his learning the numbers and doing it himself, is more important than getting the job done.

Ten-year-old William will attend school for the first time tomorrow. The father will earn a living with a donated sewing machine. He is ready to apply his ambition and energy to work hard and become independent.

It inspires me to work with hopeful people. They love to learn practical things, and the work goes well with many hands helping.

At the end of such days, one is almost completely exhausted. Yet, one becomes so energized by such events, even in the lives of others, that we begin to realize that these are the experiences that make us truly alive.

I remember three weeks ago, when together we faced the desperation, and humiliation of their poverty in the street where we found them. I remember the kids, the hunger, and the burning fevers, the desperation written on the face of the mother, the father's shame of failure.

Now the father of this family will work hard, and a sewing machine is best for him because he has only one arm and one leg. He doesn't even think of himself as handicapped, and he was very handy at getting around and helping during the building of the house.

They will be independent soon. They are healthy, busy, and hopeful already...

I explained to the eight-year-old Angela, "You will be going to school, too, in a few days, and you will have a godmother who will pay for your education, and maybe write letters to you once in awhile." She just listened intently and nodded her head in agreement without a word. Later as we continued with the building, we noticed her sitting on a pile of boards crying and she couldn't stop and we couldn't get from her what was wrong.

When her mother returned a little later, her mother explained to us, "Nothing is wrong, but Angela was just so overjoyed about going to school that she got very emotional about that, and having a house to live in, and a bed to sleep in." Although Her crying was because she was overwhelmed, it looked like ordinary crying to me. The reason for the tears was that now all of little Angela's secret wishes had suddenly been granted, and besides all of that, she would be getting a new sponsoring godmother!

There are many more victims of poverty in the streets. All they usually need is a hand up. They have the desire and ambition but lack the opportunity or the tools or the training to do it by themselves. The ones we have found are troubled, they are hungry and broken, but continue to struggle to hold their families together.

When I see such hungry and broken people I sometimes ask, "So... where's the agency that's supposed to take care of them? Who's running the program for them?"

Then I realize... "Perhaps *we're* the program!" I often shutter to think about such an awesome responsibility we have, when these poorest of God's people often look to us as their only hope.

And I worry about how many I may have missed, as they pass by in the street.

Chapter 47

Serendipity

"I think you might have the gift of 'serendipity,'" a volunteer told me once when we were working together.

"Yeah, maybe," I answered. "But, why do I have to have a gift with such a silly name?"

"I've been told that I can figure a way to do things sometimes. But, I think maybe we all have some of that," I remarked.

It's true that I can often find unusual ways to solve problems. It came in handy once driving the four-wheel drive on a back mountain road. Lots of things can go wrong, especially where there is no one to help. When things go wrong in the mountains, one has to figure a way out of trouble.

Once on one of those back roads, I saw a little steam forming on the windshield. I quickly shut off the engine because I figured we must have been losing water from the radiator.

"Is that water?" I asked Pedro. "Why is there water there on the windshield?"

Hopping out of the jeep, he rubbed it between his fingers. "Yeah, it's water all right," he answered.

We lifted the hood. It was bad news because the top radiator hose had sprung a leak and steam was blowing out of a little hole there. "I wonder how much water we've lost?" I questioned.

"The gauge shows a little hot," he said looking inside, "and the altimeter says seven thousand feet," he added. Then he came around the front again and asked, "Want any more information?"

"So what will we do now?" I asked. "We have to wait until it cools down now," I said, answering my own question. We should have carried a better set of tools with us. All we had was about a yard of barbed wire, but no duct tape. "How can we even drive without duct tape?" I thought.

"There is a hacksaw and a pliers on the floor of the back seat," Pedro announced.

"There is no water around here," he said, "we're up too high."

"We've got enough water if we don't lose any more," I said. "But we've got to be careful. If we drive with that hole in the radiator hose, we will lose all of our water and really overheat."

We sat for a while on some rocks beside the jeep looking at it. If wishing could have fixed it, we'd have been on our way. I think we were just pretending that we were waiting for the jeep to cool down, but we really hadn't figured out yet what to do.

Then I noticed the tail pipe, and got an idea.

"Pedro," I said, "what if we used the hacksaw to cut a few inches off the tail pipe?" I saw a little disappointment in his face as I spoke, as if he thought I had been sitting in the sun too long.

"No, wait," I said. "We could cut the radiator hose off, too, where the little hole is!" His face looked a little frightened now I thought.

"So, how does that help us to get home?" he asked, very seriously now, probably hoping it was only a temporary brain cell malfunction that I was having.

"We could put the piece of tail pipe like a splice in the radiator hose that we cut apart," I began, "and then we could untwist the barb wire and use pieces of the wire instead of clamps. We have a pliers to twist the ends of the strands of wire to tighten it around the radiator hose so it won't leak."

He raised his chin a little and narrowed his eyebrows like he always did when he was thinking. "Go over that again," he said in his quiet thinking voice.

I walked around the jeep explaining, and showing in detail what we would use and how we would do it. I could tell by his face that he "got it" and we set to work doing it. Sawing off the tailpipe was the most work, and then the rest was easy to do.

"I'll cut the radiator hose off where the leaky place is," I said, "and you can slip your little piece of tail pipe in between there, and then we'll tighten up the wire clamps with the pliers."

"You get to tell every one the story when we get home," I told him, once we were on our way again, "and you can explain it to the mechanic, too." And then we got to laughing at ourselves... making our cooling water run through our exhaust pipe like that.

Who ever heard of such a thing?

Chapter 48

Camera Borrower

"Can I borrow your camera?" a man asked me one morning. It seemed unusual for a person unknown to me, to knock on my door, and ask to borrow my camera.

I turned to ask the house girls, who were looking to see who had knocked, "Do you know this person?" I asked.

"Yeah, yeah, he's OK," one of the girls said. So I handed the man my camera and he went away with it.

After a few hours there was another knock on the door. "Thanks for letting me borrow your camera," said the man handing it back to me, "I really appreciate it."

That same thing happened three or four more times during the next month. It was the same person, and each time he returned my camera after four or five hours. My curiosity about this camera borrowing began to grow. "What is he doing that he needs to borrow my camera every once and awhile?" I wondered.

"Who is that man who borrows my camera all the time?" I asked the house-girls one day after he returned my camera and rushed off. "I never get a chance to talk to him because he is always in a hurry."

"We thought you were going to ask us pretty soon," one of the girls said. "He has a tiny shop down in the village main street."

"Oh," I said, "that explains it! What kind of a shop?"

"It's a photo shop... He takes people's pictures," the other one explained. "That's how he makes a living."

"Why does he need my camera?" I asked.

"Because he takes people's pictures... I just told you," said the girl giggling. "It works better when you use a camera."

"So," I pursued, "what's wrong with his camera?"

"Oh," said Monica, "he doesn't have a camera. He can't afford one, so he borrows yours once in a while."

"How can he run a business like that, if he doesn't have a

camera?" I wanted to know.

"Well," said Ana, "he borrows cameras from about twelve different people so he doesn't bother any one person too much."

"And now you get to be on his list," Monica informed me. "It's probably an honor!"

The next time I was in the States, I stopped at a Savers Store, found a pretty nice camera for four or five dollars, and stuck it in my bag when I returned to Guatemala. I had also clipped a two-by-two inch picture of a couple of monkeys out of a *National Geographic* magazine. These I put inside the camera so I could pull them out later as if it were an instant Polaroid.

All I had to do was to wait for the camera guy to knock on my door. In a few days he was there knocking.

"Can I borrow your camera?" came the request.

"I was in the States and I picked up a camera that I'm going to give you," I said. "Can you wait here a moment?"

"This camera is different than the other one," I said. "Watch, I'll show you how it works."

"Monica, Ana," I called, "could you two pose for me for a minute. I want to show this gentleman something." So, I pretended to take their picture together, counted to ten, opened the camera, and handed the picture of the two monkeys to the camera guy.

When they heard the camera guy laugh, the two girls came rushing to see their picture. It was pretty funny from my point of view at least.

Chapter 49

My Backpack Book

"You really like spinach, don't you?" I asked Sister Maria Kimball. "You like it a lot, right?"

"Yes, I admit that I eat a lot of spinach," she confessed.

"I found little spinach patches all over down on the farm," I said. "Do you even know where those patches you planted are anymore? I asked.

"No, I run into patches I've forgotten all the time," she said.

"So, why don't you plant something I like, like raspberries or something good," I asked, "instead of those old weeds you grow?"

Once in a while I'd bring a bunch of spinach to her nunnery for her, and she brought some raspberries for me a few times. Maria was a very good friend. This North American School Sister of Notre Dame cared deeply for the children who came to her for care.

"Tell me about Dorothy Day," I said to her on a village street corner as we sat on some boulders talking. "What was she like?" I asked.

"I was her companion on the streets of New York for a long time," she told me. Maria related stories about their experiences that I'm sure were never recorded. What an interesting lifestyle that must have been. "I was with her when she died," she said, and then Maria told me about that experience, too.

"What kind of stuff did Dorothy Day like to read?" I asked once.

"Oh, she read lots of things," Maria answered. "But there was one special book she liked to read. It was a meditation book about faith. I don't recall the name of it, but she carried it with her everywhere she went."

My expression must have changed a little at hearing that.

"What's the matter?" she asked, noticing a change in my continence. I explained that it was nothing, but that I had a favorite book too, that was a meditation about faith. I also told her that I take it with me wherever I go, because I thought it had made an impact on my life and work.

"It's a book that nobody ever reads, and no one has ever heard about," I told her.

"So what is the name of the book you read," she asked. So, I fished it out of my bag and handed her the worn copy of my book.

"This is the exact same book!" she said surprised.

Later, as I was thinking about it, I thought that maybe this is a dangerous book. Perhaps I shouldn't let others read it because there may be something about it that might affect people's lives somehow. Maybe I should stop reading it myself.

About a year later, six months after Sister Maria Kimball had returned to Maryland, I encountered three Sisters of Charity working in a very poor section of Guatemala City. They were telling me about the time they met Mother Teresa, who was the head of their community.

It was interesting to hear their first-hand account of meeting Mother Teresa. "She is a very ordinary and humble person," they all agreed, "She has a way of inspiring people." They told me many things about her, including about the book she took with her everywhere.

I was afraid to ask, so I just dug out my worn copy from my backpack and handed it to them. They looked at it, surprised, and wanted to know how I knew…

"It's the very book she kept with her," they said.

That's when I thought it best to put a plain brown wrapper on my copy of the book, in case someone might accidentally read the title and go out and get a copy of their own as I had.

Chapter 50

Village Square Chickens

One morning Monica had just brought me a plate of poached four-minute eggs when several men knocked on our door.

"Who can that be?" we all asked. "Who would come knocking before six in the morning?" Then Monica walked over and opened the door. There were four men. They must have come into the village on the early bus. She turned to look at me, saw my hand motion and led them in.

"Welcome gentlemen," I said to them as I shook their hands. "Sit down here at the table." Then without asking them, I said to Monica, "Do up some more eggs... eight of them..." and to the other girl, "start toasting up some more bread."

The girls brought coffee and sugar to get them started. We knew that they came in on the early bus and they would be hungry.

"Where have you come from and what are your names?" I asked them. Then I wrote their names into a fresh page of my notebook in between bites of breakfast and sips of coffee.

"How many people live at 'Santo Tomas,'" I asked them.

"Maybe three of four thousand people," said one of them, a very heavy person who was built like a wrestler.

I soon learned that this was a delegation, sent to us by the people of their village. They wanted to have more protein available to the people in their village and they thought they could do this by raising chickens.

"But you must have some chickens in your village already," I said, "because lots of people have 'patio chickens' in every village."

"The few chickens that run around loose grow too slow and take more feeding than they are worth," another of the men explained. "We need a way of raising chickens so people can do it profitably. A family down on the coast showed us their chicken cages, and told us about the way you train people to raise chickens."

"So tell me the rest of your plan," I said. "How will you get this done?"

"Our hope is that you might teach the four of us today, and we would write everything down and then teach the others in our village who want to learn." said the quiet one in the plaid jacket.

"OK. We would be happy to do it that way," I said to them. "We will teach you all that we know about raising chickens today, and you can take notes. We will give you copies of the charts we use for mixing feed."

"We can give them copies of the 'cost-profit' sheets, too," suggested Pedro.

"Pedro will help teach you," I said. "He knows a lot about raising chickens at a good profit."

"But what would you think if we were to drive to your village and set up a cage in your village square?" I thought aloud. "That way we could kick off your project by doing the first cage where all can come and see how it's done!"

"And you four would be the experts to answer everybody's questions." I said as they laughed and began pointing at one another to indicate who would be the expert.

We spent the morning teaching them, showing them, and repeating the part about protein and feed mixing over and over. They wrote in their notebooks, asked questions, and drew pictures and designs of the cages. In the afternoon, we had them help build cages, do hands-on feed mixing, fill up the feeders and flip the water jugs over so the birds could drink. Now they were all experts.

They left for their return bus, notebooks in hand, and with instructions to have about fifty pounds of corn ground-up and ready. We would see them on the appointed day next week.

Our jeep was full when Annie and I set out for Santo Tomas, which was on the other side of the volcano from where we lived. Annie, my daughter who was volunteering, helped load the jeep with the cage, feeders and waters, a hand corn grinder, the box of baby chicks, and a little one-bulb heater in case they had electricity in their village.

"Do we have everything?" I asked as we sat in the jeep thinking about things we might have forgotten.

"Wait!" she said suddenly. "We forgot the kitchen sink!"

That meant that we had everything. So we set out on what seemed to be a very long road. Most of the road was driving over rough rock, but the jeep steadily climbed up the other side of the volcano.

"What on earth is that squeaking?" asked Annie. "It sounds like it's coming from the engine!" We kept driving and listening to the strange sound.

"It is coming from the engine and it is getting much louder," I said. "Don't you think so?" We listened. It was definitely much louder. "Maybe I should stop, and we should look under the hood. It sounds like a fan belt to me." We stopped and lifted the hood. It wasn't the fan belt because it was going around very normally.

"Did you look at the temperature gauge?" she asked. But the temperature was normal.

We drove some more, but the screeching kept on. All the gauges were normal. Then I tried the brakes, because we had been climbing and hadn't used the brakes since the screeching noise began. The brakes were fine. What a mystery... We didn't want to ruin our engine out in this desolate place either.

"Let's stop and take a closer look at the engine," I suggested. So we stopped and I turned off the engine. The screeching continued even with the engine turned off! "This is impossible," we said as we walked around the jeep only to realize that there were some birds sitting in the nearby trees, making that horrible loud wailing and screeching sound. What a joke on us!

Soon we were on our way again, and it wasn't long before we were driving into the little village. We figured that we only had about three hours of work time there, before we would have to head home, to get back before dark.

"Welcome," the townspeople were saying, as they gathered around our little jeep. In minutes there was a crowd. The word was out. "There will be an eleven o'clock show today in the village square."

We were sufficiently greeted by the villagers.

The four "experts" were there, too, and they showed us where to set up the cage in the square. Every child in town must have been there, with their little hands itching to touch those cute little yellow chicks. There was an endless peaking into the little

holes in the cardboard chick-box.

When they brought the corn out, they only had ground about twenty pounds. They apologized for this lack.

"Why is the corn in many different little plastic bags?" I asked puzzled, "and why is some of the corn white, some black, and some yellow?"

"Because there is no hand grinder in our village, we divided up the grinding work among quite a number of families," they explained. "We rubbed the corn between the flattest rocks that we could find to grind it."

When I reached into the jeep and pulled out the hand corn grinder we had brought for them, it brought the village square down with applause. We appointed a ten-year-old to be the cage caretaker. I explained the system of growing chickens...

Annie was sitting on an open grassy spot with a large number of little children and the box of baby chicks. She was having them take turns touching or petting the little chicks. It was a task without end.

That was their beginning of growing chickens for them. Many people in the village visited the little cage to take measurements. Many of the villagers made their cages of wood, bamboo, or wire in their back yards.

Ten days later we went back to that village for a session on giving shots and debeaking. The four "experts" were there for their hands-on session as the rest of the villagers watched. The biggest fellow, the one who was built like a wrestler, could hardly bring himself to cut off the beak of the little chick when it came his turn.

After much hesitation and many suffering faces, this strong, burley, gentle man finally debeaked the little chick. That's when we led the applause, and everyone laughed and applauded.

Chapter 51

First Shoes

There are some villages in the mountains, which cannot be seen. One can actually be in the middle of a village without knowing it. Only one house can be seen at a time. People live high up along winding trails that intersect and rise steeply and branch out in many directions.

I found myself in one such village where the end of the road for my jeep ended hundreds of feet below. I was looking for some families to arrange the school registration for their children. There were no street numbers or mailboxes with names on them. I saw house numbers, but these numbers had nothing to do with the location of the house.

So I ask, "Where does the Lopez family live?" …and quickly learn that there are too many Lopez families to have any idea of where.

"The father's name is Antonio," I add, thinking they will know immediately. No one ever heard of him because everyone uses a nickname and the people never know the real names of their neighbors. I say thanks, and begin to leave when they ask what the mother's name is, and I answer, "Maria," which gets me nowhere because sixty percent of the women there are named 'Maria.'

When I walk back down to the jeep, I notice a group of women washing their baskets of clothing at the public cement water tank nearby.

"So, why is your water level so low in the tank?" I ask them.

"Because it's the dry season," one of them said.

"The tank fills up during the night when no one is here using the water," added another, "but the water runs so slow that it takes all night to trickle the tank full."

The woman on the other side of the tank said, "If we got down here earlier there would be more water, but we're just slow." And they all laughed together at that.

"I'm trying to find some particular families to arrange school for some of their children." I said, "but I can't find where they live." Then I added, "I'm not able to find their houses up on the trails."

A woman, who was filling her water container at the tank, said her ten-year-old daughter might show me where that Lopez family lived. I hired her daughter to show me where all of the families lived who were on my list. She knew all of the other children on the mountain, so she helped me find all of the families I was looking for. So… she led me back up the trail... right up where I had already been. Antonio Lopez lived only a few doors away from where I had been asking directions earlier.

I got most of the paperwork done for the children on my list for their first day in school, which would be the day after tomorrow. I gave them school supplies and coached the children about what school might be like for them. They were all very excited.

Contacting these families took most of the afternoon.

My guide's name was "Aura" and she knew where everyone lived in those mountains. She had on a very raggedy dress that was very torn and stained. She seemed like a bright child, and very social, jabbering with everyone we met.

"Would you like to go to school, too?" I asked Aura when we had finished with the others.

Her eyes brightened and her head nodded immediately. "I have to ask my mom," she said. I had met her mother earlier filling her water jug.

"So, where do you live?" I asked. She just pointed up… and so we had to walk clear to the top of the mountain trail because they lived in the uppermost house of the tiny village.

Her mother was excited by the idea and told me the sad tale of their low station in life and how sending her two girls to school was beyond her dreams. That's when I discovered that there was another daughter who was eleven named Belkis. It was beginning to get dark, so I arranged to meet the mother and both daughters the next day at about two in the afternoon down at the water tank. Then we would make the rest of the arrangements.

"We laid on our corn mats that night and could hardly sleep," the girls told me much later. "We couldn't believe that we were really going to school and learn to read and write."

The next day we did school registration paperwork, and then

went to the open market and got the school supplies they would need. I also got them each a school bag to carry their stuff to school and back every day. It must have been like nothing they had ever experienced. They wanted to know how to write their names right away…

I took out my Swiss army knife and sharpened a new pencil for each of them. I showed them how to write their names on their new tablets, and they tried to practice as we bumped along the cobblestone streets in the jeep.

"Now it's time for dresses and shoes," I announced as their eyes widened with excitement. It was a grand time picking out dresses and shoes. Even their mother couldn't keep up with them.

I'll never forget Aura almost walking into a large basket of tomatoes. I grabbed her just before she went headfirst in. They had never had shoes on their feet before!

The problem was that they were walking, while at the same time looking at their feet from the side. There was no mirror and they wanted to see how very cute their feet looked walking in those new black shoes! That's when they began walking into things!

I think we were all exhausted. They each had a pair of new shoes, two new frock dresses, lots of pencils and tablets and other school supplies.

By the time we finished it was lightly raining, and by the time we got out of the market and headed back up to their village the rain was already drumming on the roof of the jeep. It would now be dark before we could all get home.

I turned on the jeep lights and the windshield wipers. The girls were in the back seat and they were singing, noisy, and giddy. We had been climbing and winding with the jeep approaching their particular mountain. It was then that I noticed the reflection of their mother's face in the flat windshield made visible by the bright dash lights.

Streaming tears were rolling down her cheeks.

"Are you alright?" I asked. And she told me it was only her joy at seeing her girls so happy. They would live the dream that had been her own dream for herself when she was their age.

And that's how it was as we drove up towards their one-room dirt floor house of cane high on the volcano.

Chapter 52

The Family Trap

There is an abandoned house on a back street in one of the villages, where there are only two adjacent adobe walls left standing. It's a corner formed by two six-foot walls without a roof.

I named this place, "The Family trap"

It's in one of the poorest mountain villages. I have found many abandoned families there when things got really bad for them. As life continues to beat them up, they sort of end up hunkered in by these two walls still clinging on to whatever is left. I can always see from two blocks away when a family has moved into that spot…

They put food and things on top of those two walls so dogs can't get at it.

Late one afternoon I found a widow with five children living there. They had been deserted. They were mostly sick by the time I found them. I asked them if they needed something.

"We need some blankets," Julia said, "because we only have three, and they are worn and threadbare." So I loaded her and all of her children into my jeep and we drove to our village and the project house for three more blankets. I also gave them some bread and some high protein cereal.

Then I brought them back to their "house" in the small village where they lived. The mother, Julia, seemed to be in a hurry now, so I decided to leave and come back the next day. As I headed back to my jeep, though, she surprised me by asking me for a ride back to the larger village from which we had just come.

"Myself and all of my children, too," she said.

"But why?" I asked, "would you go there when it's already almost dark?" It was puzzling. "How will you get back home in the dark later with all those children?" I asked.

"I have to go to work," she said simply, "and I have to take all five of my children with me because I can't leave them alone."

So into the jeep they all piled again. When we got to the larger village, I asked her where she worked and she just told me to stop anywhere along the street. She got all of the children out and parked them on the curb and started down towards the door of a very nice house.

"Is this where you work?" I asked, "and what about the children?" The oldest was about twelve. That's when she told me her story…

"I go knocking on doors," she said, "until someone gives me work washing clothes by hand or doing some ironing or any kind of cleaning chores. Then after a couple of hours, they pay me a couple of dollars," she continued. "Then I go to a store where I buy whatever food I can for what money I have earned."

"I gather up my children then," she continued, "and we walk home those four miles in the dark. Then we gather some wood to make a fire, make tortillas and eat whatever we were able to buy, before we go to sleep in that corner," she said. Then she went up and knocked on the door of a house, and soon disappeared inside.

Two hours later, when she came out, I was still there on the street with those children. I drove them all to a store, and then back to their two walls for the night. She was a very brave woman barely keeping body and soul together. And tomorrow it would be the same, but without the jeep rides.

So… that's how I found them. They had a long way to go, but conditions like these are often where we begin with a family's development.

And soon, even before we get them settled in a safe place, and trained in a good job, and the children all in school…

…I'd find another family there, living where those two walls meet in the corner. It was a family trap. It was the place to be… if you're looking for the poorest of the poor.

Chapter 53

Restaurant Ritual

"Do you have hamburgers?" I asked the waitress.

"No, there are no hamburgers," she said. "It's on the menu there, but we don't have any today."

"Then I'll have some eggs with toast," I said.

"We don't have any eggs and there is no bread today," said the waitress, waiting for an alternative choice.

"Then I'll have some ham with any vegetable you have," I said, continuing to play the guessing game.

"I can bring some black beans... Is that alright for the vegetable?" she asked.

"What about the ham?" I asked.

"Let me check on that," she said and left. We waited for a long time.

Soon the waitress walked in the front door from outside, and came to our table and announced, "There is no ham today."

"Pork chops?"

"No."

"Chicken?"

"Would you like the dinner or the sandwich?" she asked.

"I'd like the sandwich, but there is no bread," I offered.

"So do you want the dinner with one piece of chicken or two?" she asked.

"Two pieces of chicken will be fine," I answered.

The others with us, decided to have chicken, too. "Watch," I said to the others who were working with us that day. "In a few minutes that little girl over there by the kitchen will go walking out of the door with that basket swinging beside her."

Then, in a few minutes the little girl spoke with her mother from the kitchen, and took the basket and swung it beside her as she left through the door.

"How did you know that she would do that?" asked the lady

who was with us. "If you're such a prophet, tell us where she went."

"Oh, I'm not a prophet," I said, "but she will be back as soon as she goes to the market and buys enough chicken and black beans for our meals. That will take about twenty minutes. It will then take about thirty or forty minutes to cook everything and serve it. If you add in the guessing game, and the time we need to finish eating, almost two hours will have passed.

"There must be better restaurants around," said a man who was with us.

"There are only five restaurants in this village, and two of them only serve sandwiches," I said, "and this one is the best one in town."

Then I told the little girl's mother in the kitchen, that we would be back in about forty minutes to eat. All four of us went back to where we had been sanding school desks and painting them with waterproofing sealer. We worked another hour before diner.

"When you're in that restaurant," I told them as we worked, "if you order chicken, they send out for eggs, hatch them, raise the chicken, then serve it to you. On the other hand, if you order eggs, they send out for a baby chick, raise that up to be a hen, wait for it to lay some eggs, then they serve them to you!"

"Which came first then, the chicken or the egg?" laughed the lady with us.

"Neither," said the man, "they both came last!"

Much later while we were in the restaurant beginning to eat our chicken dinners, I told them of the old Mayan beggar woman who often comes into the restaurants to beg food away from the customers. She asks for some of your food. If you give her some of your food, she blesses you. If you say, "No!" she will put a curse on you.

I no sooner finished speaking, when suddenly this beggar woman was standing in the doorway of the restaurant. She was an old woman with white disheveled hair and a cackle in her voice. She appeared suddenly as did Macbeth's witches on the heath. We were the only customers in the restaurant, so we were in for it. Then she saw us, got a cynical smile on her face, and started towards us.

We were soon to become part of her retirement food program.

I went to the next table and brought in another chair as we made space for her at our table. As we sat her down, I signaled to the waitress to bring another plate. "Welcome, come and sit down." I said to the old woman.

"You will be our guest today," I continued. "We have food to share with you today. There is no waiting in this restaurant for special guests."

She had surprised us all, I think, but no one was as surprised as the old beggar woman.

Chapter 54

Nutrition Center

"Please don't take the child home yet!" said Sister Maria, pleading with the child's mother. "It's too soon to take him home yet."

"But he looks so much better," said the mother, "and now he is beginning to gain weight again. He looks so much better than he was when I brought him in."

"He is heavier because we have been feeding him good foods with high proteins and vitamins," responded Maria. "Will you be able to feed him so that he will keep gaining?"

"I think so," said the child's mother. "We have food at our house. He eats all he wants."

"But corn tortillas alone are not enough for a little child like this," argued Sister Maria. "He needs things like eggs and meat so he can be healthy."

"Oh, but we have meat really often," claimed the mother.

"You do?" asked Maria puzzled, thinking about why the child ended up in the nutrition center. "Well, how often do you have meat, and does the little boy eat much of it?"

"Yes," responded the mother. "He loves to eat meat, and he eats all he wants. We have meat almost every day."

"Really?" asked Maria puzzled again. "What kind of meat do you have at your house?"

"We have squash!" she said with a smile, "and he just loves it."

"So you think the problem with most nutrition centers," I said to Sister Maria later, "is that the mothers come to take their children home too soon."

"Yes," Maria said. "The child goes back to the same conditions that he came out of, and there the child begins to lose weight a second time… and then there is no turning them around to a gaining condition again, and they most often die."

"What if the mothers get more involved in what the nutrition center does?" I asked. "If they would learn to actively help to get their own child gaining weight again at the center, wouldn't they do the same thing later at home?"

"That's a good idea," said Maria. "But we would have to teach every mother how to be a nutritionist."

"Maybe that's our work. This is good information, Sister Maria," I said, "because we will soon be building six new nutrition centers in the next village."

That was the beginning of a new concept in nutrition centers. Soon we began building the six nutrition centers in the next village, and training the workers who would be in charge of them. In just a few months, we had the first nutrition center up and running.

One day, after one of the centers had been operating for a month or so, I invited Sister Maria to come there with me to see what she might think of this new concept.

"You're building them of corn canes!" Sister Maria said in a surprised voice. "It looks just like the cane houses the people live in." It's true! We were building cane buildings for our nutrition centers, although they did have a cement floor. We wanted them to look like the homes of the poorest of the people we wanted to help.

"We don't have big white refrigerators, or gas stoves, or flushing toilets either," I announced as I took Maria on a tour of the finished nutrition center. "All we have is a wood cook stove just like they do in their homes. We didn't bother to install electricity in these centers either," I added.

"Are you sure this is a good idea?" she asked.

"Well, we have one hard and fast rule: that the mothers must bring the child every morning, and get the child every evening. That way the child can sleep at home. The mothers must come to volunteer for a half day twice each week," I explained. "They are the ones who do the cooking and feeding.

"What if they don't come?" she asked.

"Then we send the child home," I said, "and we tell them that it's better for the child to die at home! It hasn't been a problem. The mothers don't mind coming to help, because they feel at home here."

"But how can you run a nutrition center without refrigera-

tion?" asked the Sister, shaking her head.

"When these mothers feed their children in their homes, they don't have refrigerators!" I said. "So, now they have no excuses anymore. They can't say: 'You have a refrigerator,' or 'You have a tile floor', or 'a gas stove', or 'canned food', or whatever…"

"Let's go with them to the market, Maria," I suggested. "They're just getting ready to leave. Let's tag along behind and watch what they do."

Every morning the little group of mothers go with the director of the nutrition center to the open market and buy only what they need for the day. "They don't buy squash, even though it's cheap and tasty. The protein content of squash is almost zero," I pointed out. "They buy carrots, but not radishes. They buy only a little chicken, or once in awhile they buy turkey because these are cheaper meats. They prefer turkey because the protein is higher and the fat is lower."

"This is like a 'market school' for the volunteer mothers," said Maria. "They always seem to check with the director about everything before they pay for it."

"Most of them don't do numbers very well, and some of the sellers cheat them," I explained as we watched one of the women counting her change. "So we teach those mothers who do not read, to make change by the colors of the bills, and the sizes of the coins."

"I can't understand what they're saying, because they are speaking the local dialect!" said Maria.

"Most of the uneducated women speak very poor Spanish," I said. "That's why our center directors must not only speak the dialect of the women who come, but they must also dress like the women who bring their children. If they are nurses they cannot wear white."

"Well, I'm a nurse," said Sister Maria, "and I wouldn't be qualified to work here then... because I speak a different dialect."

"That's right. And, they won't let me work in the center either," I said laughing, "because they're afraid they may have to eat some of my cooking."

"What do you do when the mothers want to take the child home before they are safely gaining again?" she asked, thinking about her problem with the woman who thought that squash was meat.

"Well, they have the child home every night," I said, "and they do the weight charting on their own children here at the center... so they know when they are ready."

"This place is more of a school than a nutrition center," observed Maria.

"Many of them bring their children back in for a weight check now and then," I said. "We've learned that it's better to teach them, than do things for them."

Chapter 55

Blind Vision

"My name is Irene," she said. "I am from the coastal lands." That was the young woman's first introduction to us. She was sixteen years old and she was blind.

We came to know Irene very well. She lived with us at our house for a number of months. She had an eye operation and had received corrective glasses and had recently gained her vision. The doctor said her vision was almost normal now.

"She does not know how to use her new vision," the doctor had said. "You have to teach her how to see. She had never been able to see before."

"Don't people naturally figure out how to use their new eyesight?" I asked. "Wouldn't she just begin looking at everything, and be amazed at the colors and what things look like?" For her the answer was "No."

For all practical purposes, she was still blind.

"Look at the cup when you pick it up, Irene," I would say, but she would be looking elsewhere. Then she would feel along the table for the cup. When she found the cup, and before picking it up, she would feel with her finger to see how full of coffee or water the cup was.

"I don't know how!" she would say. "This is very hard to do."

It was like she had two lazy eyes. Never in her life before did she ever have to use her eyes and focus them on anything. "This is a lot of work," she would say.

We had to make it into a game. "Pick up that spoon, Irene, without touching the table," I said, knowing that she couldn't feel along the surface of the table with her hand to find the spoon. This seemed to work. "You use your eyes only when you have to," I accused her.

"Teach me to speak English!" she asked me quite often when she overheard us speaking English. "Please?" she would beg.

"No, Irene, you speak Spanish, but you need to learn to read and write in Spanish first," I often told her. "Then you can learn another language."

"Please!" she would say. "Teach me a few words."

Then I got an idea! I've been looking for something to give her as a reward for using her eyes when we practice. "Why couldn't I teach her English words as rewards when we work on her vision games?" I asked myself.

"Irene," I said, "whenever you do well in your vision exercises, I will teach you one English word. If you do badly, I will not teach you any new words." Then she wanted to do the vision games right away. "Maybe I've opened a Pandora's box," I thought.

The first word she learned in English was "cup." I only taught her one word, because I thought it best to keep her a little hungry so she would work harder on her vision. I had some second thoughts about this whole plan anyway. She jabbered constantly in Spanish, so maybe it wasn't good to give her a second language when one language was too much sometimes.

"That is a 'table,'" I taught her. "That is a 'chair' setting over there. These are your 'glasses,'" I said, touching her new glasses.

"You lying!" she said, "Yesterday you said that 'glasses' are what we drink water out of." Later I proved to her with one of the volunteers that I had not lied, so she asked forgiveness. She was very religious.

I taught her well, and she learned fast... except for one word that I taught her wrong. I probably shouldn't have but I thought she had it coming.

One day she wanted to know what the word was for "sugar" that was in the sugar bowl. It was there on the table where we were doing exercises.

"You haven't earned a word!" I answered, "so, I won't tell you." Then the begging started and it really interrupted our work. So I said, "that stuff is called 'crap'" and she learned it just that quick. I was perfectly justified because she had already called me a liar.

Her vision did improve slowly, and as she learned to see, she got more and more excited about seeing things. Once I read her the story of the man born blind from my Spanish Bible, and she really identified with the man and his newly found vision.

She was about finished with the training, and ready to go back to her home on the coast. Then Father Phil came by for a visit one evening from the other side of the village. Irene decided to put out some cookies and show-off with her limited English in serving some lunch.

"Have a cookie?" she asked in her halting English, putting the plate of cookies on the table. It went pretty good, and she was so proud. Then she offered him a cup of coffee and innocently inquired whether or not he would care for a little "crap" in it.

Phil and I were both lucky we didn't each end up with a hernia, and somehow I survived Irene's wrath, too, when she learned the word should have been "sugar," and that the slang meaning for "crap" was practically a sin for her to say.

Chapter 56

Jeep Driving Lessons

We appointed Sister Maria as the spiritual director of our house. She was a nurse and a nutritionist. She was born in a village about an hour's drive away. She was not a driver.

"David," she would always say, "teach me to drive the jeep!"

"When there is time," I would say to her, "I will try to find time." I had her drive about a half block once. She couldn't figure which way to turn the steering wheel to turn left. I could teach her to drive, I thought, but I might endanger too many people in the process.

"Today," she said, "today would be good... when I finish at the nutrition center..."

"I'll do it sometime," I laughed, "when I think I need more pain in my life!"

She thought she could learn to drive by watching me drive. That's why she accompanied me to the villages sometimes. "Why do you do this?" she would ask. "Why do you do that? She would ask. She was constantly reporting my speed to me. It was a little unnerving.

I paid her back as I drove by doing things for her to watch that had no meaning whatsoever. Once in a remote village, I was talking to her as I cruised through a street intersection a little fast...

"David, you didn't look to see if something was coming! Did you?"

"No, I didn't look," I said. "Why? Is that important?"

"Yes, it's important. We could have been killed!" she said.

"No Maria," I explained, "There is only one car in this village... and we are in it! Explain to me how we could hit that one car that is in this village, and that we are inside of."

Eventually it happened that during a weak moment I may have promised to begin giving her driving lessons. "We will begin by having you practice washing the jeep," I announced. "Then we will have you rotate the tires."

"In your dreams," she said, arms folded.

We went out on the soccer field to begin with basics. "First we are going to teach you steering. When you learn that, we can practice on some of the back streets."

We spent the whole afternoon practicing a very simple concept, "Turn the wheel to the right, when you want to turn right." When she just couldn't grasp that, I tried another concept.

"Turn the wheel to the left, when you want to turn left, Maria" It just wasn't working. "Tell me what you are thinking when you want to make a turn," I said finally.

"When you say to turn left," she began, "I never can remember if I should move the top of the wheel to the left... or the bottom of the wheel to the left." I really tried very hard to keep a straight face as the inside of me wanted to laugh.

I got out of the jeep, went into the back, and got some red electrical tape out of my toolbox, Then I came around to the driver's side and wrapped red tape around the top of the wheel.

"See that red tape, Sister?" I asked. She nodded. "That red tape is what you move to the right or to the left." It was like the lights came on in her mind.

"Let's try it!" she said full of hope. It was like a miracle. She was now able to turn the jeep in the direction she wanted it to go every time. "Let's go and drive around the village now!" she said. But it was time to end the first lesson. Besides it was getting dark already.

A few days later I had to teach her how to shift with a clutch as she was driving. The first confusing thing for her was that there were two shift levers on the floor because it was a four wheel drive jeep. She couldn't remember if it was the big lever on the left or the shorter one on the right.

"How will I remember which one to shift?" she asked.

"Hand me that roll of red electrical tape there on the dash," I said. After awhile we weren't doing too badly. There was a lot of jerking and grinding, but I didn't worry about that, because she could learn to replace the gears and clutches.

Then we moved to the big time. We went to a small road that

wove through the little farm where there weren't many cars. It was perfect, with the fences and buildings and winding curves and short turns. "I can't remember sometimes," she said, "if I'm supposed to move the shift lever when the clutch is in or when it is out."

"You've watched me drive now for six months," I said laughing. "Just do what you saw me do thousands of times." But soon she got the hang of it a little bit. She was stopping and shifting up and then shifting down. To my surprise, she was doing these things while turning the jeep at the curves and corners in the correct direction.

Then when she was going past one of the gardens where the road curved a little to the right, she turned the wheel a little to the left. Then when the jeep didn't go to the right, she turned sharply to the left.

"Help!" was all that she yelled, as we busted through the fence that runs between the road and the gardens. There are still some vibrating echoes remaining of her yell, in those mountain canyons today. There was a loud crashing and busting sound as we entered the garden area leaving the wooden and wire fence in shambles behind us. Then there was a scraping of barb-wires that scraped over the top or got caught on the windshield and stretched as we drove over the first raised carrot bed.

I could see that we had about a dozen or fifteen raised growing beds to bounce over if we were to hit the chicken coop with any decent speed.

"Maria!" I shouted, "you've got your foot on the gas, not the brake! You can't stop by pressing on the gas! You've got to press on the brake!" She was too busy to understand me as she pulled backward on the wheel and pressed even harder on the gas. By now we were grinding up our sixth raised growing bed and bouncing toward the seventh. "Maria!" I yelled, "what do you want me to do?"

"Stop the jeep!" she yelled, "Stop the jeep!"

"OK," I yelled back and I reached up and turned off the ignition switch.

"What happened back there, Sister?" I asked.

I think that darned tape fell off of the top of the wheel!" she answered.

Then she said, "You have to drive it out of here," and started to get out.

"No," I said, "you have to drive it out."

"How am I going to get out of here? You drive it out of here."

"You have to drive it out of here," I said finally. "Because you have more experience driving in gardens than I do."

Then she backed it out over each of the raised growing beds and through the busted place in the fence. Soon we were back on the little farm road again. It was a good opportunity to teach her to use that other little shift lever when we needed to back up through those carrot beds with four-wheel drive engaged.

I was really looking forward to teaching her to drive the hairpin turns up on the mountain road.

Chapter 57

Garden Tutoring

"Everything is lined up," shouted Diego. "Lower it… slowly, slowly… OK! That's it!" The men had lowered the heavy diesel water pump onto the concrete pad.

They had to lower it carefully onto the bolts sticking up through the concrete slab. Then there was a thumping together of the poles, as the men threw them onto a pile nearby.

"Hand me another nut," said one of the men reaching out with his hand extended. In a few minutes, two other men were going around putting the final torque on the nuts and bolts, which held the large diesel engine down. The men were standing around the powerful engine, satisfied that they had done well positioning it.

"Pour in that can of diesel fuel!" I said. "Now that it's bolted tight, we're going to give it a test run to see if there is still too much vibration."

"Hook up the cables to the jeep battery," I heard someone say, as I drove the jeep up closer so the jumpers would reach.

The engine started. Then as it picked up speed, it barked a couple of times shooting puffs of black diesel exhaust billowing into the sky. The men instinctively backed up a step or two. Soon when it reached its normal pumping speed, the vibrations died away, and the engine hummed along as smooth as silk.

The large diesel pump seemed out of place. If you stepped back, you could see the blue tranquil mountain lake with the volcanoes rising high on every side mirrored in the rippled water of the lake. When the men revved it up a couple of times, the black exhaust and loud throbbing sound added to the intrusion.

They shut off the engine and the quiet tranquility of the mountain returned.

"When will we hook up the suction line in the lake?" someone asked.

They wanted to get this irrigation system going now. The irrigation pipes and the pump had been setting here idle for two years. The floating raft in the lake needed repair. Now they could see that it might get finished at last. There was an excitement in the air.

"The engine runs well," I said to the men. "Next, we need to buy the pipe adapter we need, and connect it up to the suction line. Thanks for your help this evening!"

"Remember to be here next Tuesday," I added before anyone left. "The classes in gardening will begin at about eight o'clock in the morning. Tell your neighbors, too."

There were more than two-hundred acres of land rising gently from the lake upward towards the base of the volcano. The rainfall charts I had been studying indicated that corn here could only produce about fifteen or twenty bushels per acre at best.

"We could grow five times that amount of production with irrigation," I had told them in my classes in growing corn.

This was volcanic soil. The land was rich, but lacked enough rainfall. Each family was using about one or two acres to grow their corn. I taught them to use fertilizer and inoculate their beans the year before.

"Show me the method you've been using to fertilize the corn," I said when we had walked out in the field where there were some corn stalks.

"This is how we do it," volunteered one of the men. "First, hand me that pan of fertilizer." Then he showed me how he took a handful of field dirt in his left hand, then threw in a tiny pinch of fertilizer with his right hand and mixed it together. Then he put it around the cornstalk and mixed it in a little.

"That's an interesting way to do it," I commented. "But why did you first take a handful of field dirt and mix it with only a small pinch of fertilizer?" I asked, knowing that he was using way too little fertilizer.

"Because that's how I make more fertilizer." He told me.

"We can't afford much fertilizer," said another. "We don't have much money because we get very poor yields. If the land gave us more corn, we could afford to buy more fertilizer," he added.

Now they needed ideas of what they could grow during the dry season now that they would be able to irrigate the land. Tuesday we were bringing in two gardeners, as teachers, from the village across the mountain where we lived. They would teach these men to grow vegetables on raised growing beds.

Tuesday came soon enough. "Good that you brought your hoes and shovels!" I said to a group of men walking down the broad path to the lake near the diesel pump.

"There are a lot of people here," commented one man waiting with his large hoe. Their hoes looked more like heavy flat grub axes than hoes.

"OK, lets get started," I announced when most of the men had arrived. "This is Alex. He operates a large garden in the village of San Lucas. He knows how to grow tomatoes and potatoes and herbs and medicines. He also knows how to graft fruit trees. You can ask him any questions you want."

"This is Pablo," I announced putting my hand on his shoulder, "He knows a lot about irrigation of vegetables and building raised beds of fertilized soil to grow your produce."

"These are the seeds you can use," I said pointing to the seeds stacked up on the unused part of the diesel platform. We are going to make raised garden beds and seed them in this whole area that you see roped off here," I said. "One more thing… Alex and Pablo do not speak this dialect, but they understand most of what you say."

Then I asked, "Who speaks both dialects?" There were three or four men who raised their hands, and I appointed one to Alex, and another to Pablo.

It was amazing to see how well this was working! They were communicating in three languages, and when they couldn't get the idea across in the dialects, they threw a few Spanish words in the mix. I was helpless with this mixing of languages once they got going with the hands-on work of teaching and learning.

My work was probably finished anyway, now that I had brought the resources and the teachers and the students together. The men worked throughout the whole day building and planting fifty or sixty vegetable growing beds. They had about thirty more that were ready for planting, but would not be planted for several weeks in order to spread out the harvest better. This would spread out their work more, and also give them a steady supply of products for the open markets.

Chapter 58

The Lost House

"My daughter is nine years old and I can't afford to send her to school," said a woman who came to the door with the needs and frustrations that most people express, "and she must go to school to learn reading and writing."

...and she might have added, "So she won't turn out like me; unable to read and write and unable to find decent work."

"Yes, she should go to school if it is possible," I agreed. "What is her name?"

"Her name is Claudia," she said. "Can you help her get into school?" I asked where she lived so we could get her daughter into a school in her neighborhood if possible.

"I live by the Calvary Church," she said.

"Which direction from the church?" I asked. This process is always difficult because they don't know their address or directions to their house. She couldn't read the street names or the numbers on the little street signs.

"Do you live on the road to Saint John, or on the back road to Saint Peter?" I pursued.

"Almost a block down that back road from the church," she said. "On the right side of the road... We're the only house there," she added.

That was pretty clear, I should have no trouble finding that. I drive past there every day; sometimes I pass by that road several times. "OK," I said, "I think I can find it without too much trouble." Then I wrote down some other things like the girl's birthday, which she remembered except for the year in which she was born. I learned that the woman's mother lives in their house with them, too.

In the afternoon, I drove the jeep out to see them. There was no house there. "I either got the directions wrong," I decided, "or I have gone blind." I walked over every inch of that place.

I drove back to the project house in the village. "Does anyone know where this place is," I asked everyone at the house. "I can't seem to find it." Nobody knew where it was.

I drove back there again, this time determined to find it! "Everything has to be somewhere," I thought. "There must be a rule like that." I walked through the woods on both sides of the road in case she didn't know right from left. There simply was no house there where it should have been.

As I made my last pass through the woods, I heard voices. I didn't know where they were coming from, but there were weak voices coming from somewhere. I stood still and listened. There was only a pile of brush and garbage burning nearby that I had walked by several times, but there was no house. The nearer I got to the brush and garbage pile, however, the louder the voices got.

"Oh, my!" I thought to myself, "that's their house!"

It was made of sticks and odd pieces of old cardboard, and broken boards leaned up against it here and there. Some pieces of plastic covered it to keep the rain out. There were pieces of things like bricks and stones to keep the plastic from blowing away. It was only

about four or five feet high, with smoke from their tortilla fire oozing out of a hole on the topside somewhere.

When I got up closer, I had another problem. I couldn't figure out where the door was. "Where do I knock on the door?"

"Maria, Maria!" I called out.

I soon saw the mother's face as she pulled a flap aside and looked out. "I'm glad I found you home," I said. "I need to talk to Claudia and your mother. Is there room for me inside?"

"Yes, I think so," she said. "Come in, please." I crawled in on my hands and knees. There was actually more space inside than I thought. They had small benches to sit on and it was lit inside with a candle. There was an old glass window of four panes fastened somehow on the backside to let daylight in. There was also an old tattered scatter rug on the ground.

"Good to meet you," I said to the grandmother who was there, too. "How are you?" In our conversation, she told me about her back condition and her arthritis. "It's no wonder," I thought, "sleeping on the ground and in all this dampness."

Experiences like these are where I learned some of the realities of life and the meaning of their values. I learned that there is nothing phony about the poor. They face the cold, hunger, and poverty with patience and courage.

"Here are the birth records in this box," the mother said, handing me the whole box because she was unable to read, and which I had to dig through to find the correct paper among the other things in the box.

Tomorrow we would get dresses and shoes for Claudia so she can go to school. We would get shoes for her mother, too, so she can work better. The school supplies and other arrangements with a school would be made tomorrow.

"We will also talk about putting up a better wooden house that has a cement floor so the older woman can have a regular bed to sleep in to save her back." I said. "But it will take time to get everything done."

Sometimes better housing is less expensive than the medicine people require because of unhealthy conditions. "I'd like to prescribe a chicken for some of my patients instead of medicine," one of the local doctors once said to me.

"Claudia's education should come first," said the mother, as the grandmother nodded in agreement.

"You must continue to support her and get her off to school every morning. She would have to have perfect attendance unless she is sick," I said, further explaining their part in this, "and if any of you get sick you will come to our clinic and get the medicines you need..."

"...especially for your arthritis," I said speaking to the grandmother. "Your back condition needs a good bed to sleep in, more than it needs medicine."

In a matter of weeks, some of us volunteers were able to build a small wooden house for this abandoned family there in that secluded place. There wasn't much that could be saved from their old "house" that could be reused. When they were sufficiently settled in their new house, the pile of stuff that made up their old house was finally hauled away to be burned.

Chapter 59

The Hemophiliac

Did you ever try to do the Impossible?

"I don't get it," I said to our project doctor. "If Rene is a hemophiliac, why does he have to live at the highest altitude... up where the eagles fly? Wouldn't that aggravate his condition?"

We had just received word that Rene had gotten very sick again!

We climbed up to the top of his mountain in the four-wheel drive jeep to pick him up, and take him to the Saint John of God Hospital in the capital city. His older sister came with him to take care of him in the hospital. This was not his first trip to that hospital.

"I'm going to take him home today," his father told me the next day, "Rene should be allowed to die at home up in the mountain." No argument of mine would change his mind. Rene's father had given up.

"OK," I said, "but first we must talk to Doctor Rosa Elena." His father agreed. Rosa Elena was well known by everyone in the area and especially by this family.

"If you take him home now," said Rosa Elena in her loudest authoritative doctor voice, "it would be like putting a gun to his head and pulling the trigger!"

"You must not give up yet," I said. "We need to have more time."

"OK," he said. "I will wait one more day." We would have another day to hope.

About mid-afternoon we got a call from Rene's sister who was at the hospital. "Things are not going well here," she said. "Even the doctors have little hope for his making it."

Pedro and I drove the Dodge Van into the capital city. Rene did not look good. His sister was fighting her feelings of hopelessness, while wearing her bravest mask. "There is not much that we can do for him," said the doctors. "We do not have any type A blood with which to give him a transfusion."

"What if we found some serum or plasma," I asked. "Couldn't that be given to him no matter what his blood type was?"

"Where would we get plasma?" said the doctors. "That would be impossible. It can't be done at night in the city." They had given up, too, and it was beginning to rain.

I didn't realize this would be next to impossible to accomplish in Guatemala City late at night... and in the rain. It was a good thing that I didn't know it was impossible. Rene was about eight years old and in hopeless condition. No one expected him to make it.

Two of his other brothers died when they were about his age. His father may have been right to want to take him home to die there, until I insisted that we do all that was possible.

"What are we doing?" I asked Pedro. "Are we crazy for being out here in the driving rain and darkness of Guatemala City's streets, going hospital to hospital and person to person looking for blood for Rene?" The nurses in the children's ward said I was foolish to think I could find what was needed in the city. Darkness had already settled over the city, but I still wanted to do this thing they said would be impossible.

The child grew worse. He was hemorrhaging, shaking, and white as paper. Rene clutched the little toy gift from his godparents. I could depend on Pedro. He would stay with me no matter what. We had been through other tough times together.

"Can you please help us?" I said on the phone to a hematologist whom I had finally located across the city. I was begging now.

"I have the necessary equipment," he was saying, "and I will open the lab and make what you need for your patient, no matter what the hour. You will need to bring all the donors you can find."

So we drove madly in the rain and traffic to get ice, find people, make calls, and to beg. I am sometimes glad my old friends couldn't see all that I do. I think they'd laugh to see what I have to do sometimes and how I have to beg and argue to keep life in a child.

As I drove through the darkened city, I made many stops wherever there were people. "There are some people," Pedro would say, "they look like vagabonds and street people."

"Can you give us one pint of blood to save the life of a child?" I would hear myself beg. Then I thought, "Maybe I am asking for too much!" Can I ask someone I don't know to give blood tonight in the dark and the rain of the darkened city?"

I was thinking about the paradoxical things I had read, "You want to be a leader of men? Then wash their feet! You want to save your life? Then throw it away! You want to be first? Then go to the end of the line!" We were down to the beggars and the street people. We were already at the end of the line.

Whenever someone said "yes" to our asking for blood, we were a little surprised.

We gathered as many as would fit in the van and took them with us to that lab across town. I ushered my unlikely donors into a hallway that was lined with temporary cots where the doctor drew a pint of blood from each so he could process it.

"This was a real doctor, true to his oath," I thought.

"Here is a stack of tortillas and a day's wage," I said to each of the donors as I handed the money and packages to them, "God will repay you." I know that they were expecting nothing for their efforts. Then we drove them back across the city wherever they wanted to be.

It was the middle of the night when we arrived back at the child's hospital with six or eight units of plasma packed in my ice chest. The nurses couldn't believe that we really had it. "We honestly thought you were foolish to keep trying," one nurse told me honestly, "Why did you keep going?"

"Because I didn't know it was impossible," I told her. I'm afraid I didn't give her a full and proper answer. I didn't know how to explain that I was only now learning about doing foolish things in impossible situations.

I was only beginning to discover that only when I am finally willing to do something ridiculous, can God do something miraculous.

The truth was that we were damp from the rain and worn and hungry, and still had a mountain to climb in the night to get home.

When we returned to the project that early morning, I went to visit the tomb of Saint Hermano Pedro and left a candle flickering in the blackness of that great church. I couldn't think of anything else to do.

"It's better not to look too closely at things," I thought, "...like a child going home from the hospital too soon when everyone was expecting him to die! ...and his high energy level when I drove him up to the high mountains where his family lives."

It seems that every time we set out to transform someone's life, we end up getting transformed ourselves.

Every day there are hundreds of other children with whom we connect. It's often about their shoes, and food, and houses, and health, and more. So if God wants me to go out and do something foolish, that's all right, because we're doing a number on Him too, because we have learned to finally put everything in His hands.

Chapter 60

Born on Holy Thursday

Omar didn't remember his last name.

"You don't know your last name?" I asked the young man who came to our family center one day. "That surprises me that someone doesn't have a last name."

"I lost track of my mother when I was just a wee child," he said, "and I lived with different families in different places. That's how I grew up," he added. "I got handed off to different families."

"What happened to your mother?" I asked,

"I don't remember her very much," he said. "I must have been very young when I lost track of her."

"What do your relatives say about her?" I asked. "What have they told you?"

"I don't know who any of my relatives are," he explained. "By the time I could remember things or ask any questions, the family I was with didn't even know what village I had come from."

"So, how old are you?" I asked.

"I must be about sixteen or seventeen, don't you think?" he asked. So he didn't know his age either.

"It would do no good to ask how many candles were on his last birthday cake either," I thought.

I was filling out a sheet of information about Omar because he was asking for a job. It didn't seem right that all I had on the sheet so far was "Omar" and now I wasn't too sure about that anymore.

"Do you know when your birthday is?" I asked.

"Yes, I know my birthday!" he said, looking delighted at knowing something about himself that he could tell me.

"My birthday is on Holy Thursday!" he said with certainty. "That is one of the first and only good memories I have."

Without a word I wrote "Holy Thursday" on the blank where

it said "Birthday." That seemed to please him very much. Now I had two things written on his information sheet. That was better than just one thing.

"And the year of your birth?" I asked. He didn't answer except to shake his head negatively.

"Do you know that Holy Thursday is on a different day every year?" I asked him. "And if you don't know the year of your birth, we can't figure out your birth date." I didn't really know why that was important any more. "Why can't he just have his birthday on Holy Thursday, and forget about what exact date he was born?" I asked myself, "He seems very content with that, besides if we change his birthday, his first and only good memory of himself will be ruined."

"OK, Omar," I said, "you can have a job working here with us. You can live here and occupy one of the rooms here in the project house, and you can have all of your meals here with us every day. We'll put your stuff in your room now, and then we will have some breakfast here at this table together."

So that's how Omar came to be part of our human development project here in Guatemala. He became more like a son to me than one of the workers, and he traveled with me to many of the villages where we worked. "We will go sometime to try to find some record or information about your birth," I told him one day, "and maybe even find some of your relatives." That became impossible, however, because he spoke no Mayan dialect and without that, it was too difficult to know from which part of the country he had come.

We began by teaching him to read and write in Spanish, and to do mathematics. He was a very bright young man and learned very quickly.

I taught Omar to operate the power tools in the school desk factory, and he spent many hours practicing by making things out of the scrap lumber discarded by the workers. It turned out that Omar was a very creative person with a great imagination. He had a natural sense of balance and form.

The children in the neighborhood were always happy to get his wooden toy creations. Most of the play was in the child's imagination I think. That may be where we got the idea to manufacture wooden toys for export. He also liked to laminate different kinds of wood together and turn out beautiful candle holders on the wood lathe.

He quickly learned about gardens and chickens and running the incubators. He never seemed to tire of learning how to do new things. I even taught him about photography and how to soup out photographs in our darkroom.

The greatest difficulty for him was learning to read a thermometer exactly enough. "Around seventy degrees, more or less, I think," he would say squinting at the thermometer. "Or it could be closer to seventy-five degrees, maybe," he would add. He was not very precise with the exactness of his method.

We worked pretty hard at finding out who he was and from where he had come. We just couldn't get it figured out, so I finally took him down to the Municipal office in the village and explained his situation to the village councilmen. He needed to have legal documents of identification by the age of eighteen, so now it was time to do that.

Because we had become his family, I was able to sign the papers as his guardian and he ended up with a birth date and a birthplace and a name. Omar now had legal documents, which give him an identity! Most of the information on the papers was guesswork and of his choosing, but it was all registered and official and signed now, and that's who he would be for the rest of his life. The only things he knew for certain, however, was that he was "Omar"...

...and his birthday was on Holy Thursday.

We learned years later that whenever Omar came back to visit us, he told the people wherever he was, "I'm going home to visit my family."

Chapter 61

Peace Corps Thanksgiving

From time to time I helped out at the Peace Corps training center south of the capital city. The subject of my classes usually dealt with the best means of doing production projects that fit well into the culture. Most of these were food-growing projects of one sort or another.

"Your ideas are always a great adventure for me," I said to my classes. "You are so full of innovative ideas, and that lets me see my world here with a fresh vision."

"What if we fenced in the coffee lands and had geese grazing there to save the labor of cultivation and fertilization," one of them might suggest.

"What if we mounted a chicken cage over a fish tank, to get the tank to bloom faster?" another might ask.

"Why would fish raising be a better project than planting gardens with radishes and squash? I asked.

After a lengthy discussion, they would decide that it was a matter of protein. That was correct of course. Radishes and squash have very little protein, but fish have a very high protein.

There was a guiding principle that they all learned: "It's not the technical ability of the worker that helps people make a permanent change for the better. Rather it's what one teaches the villagers that makes a permanent change."

I sat with one young woman on a mountainside overlooking the village in which she had worked for two years as a Peace Corps volunteer. She was in tears.

"I spent two years building that methane digester!" said the young woman sadly, "and they quit using it a few weeks after I left. It's just buried there now! The people never learned the principals of how to keep it working!"

"Two years of my life were wasted." She concluded. The application of technical and economic methods of production is always a problem to teach.

"I have an invitation for all of you," I announced after my last class before the Thanksgiving holiday. "We're having turkey and the trimmings for Thanksgiving at our house the day after tomorrow." Like magic, my jeep filled up with young Peace Corps volunteers for the two-hour trip back up to our house. Others came later by bus for the holiday, and we ended up pushing four big tables together for the Thanksgiving meal.

Everyone helped prepare the turkey dinner. We tried to include everyone's family tradition into the Thanksgiving celebration. Our own tradition is to pass the cranberries the wrong way around the table. To observe the tradition, the bowl of cranberries has to fight its way against all of the other serving bowls coming around the table the right way.

There was lots of table talk about their projects. "I'd like to grow fish in the lake instead of in small fish tanks," said Gary.

"Gary, how can you feed your fish if they are in the lake?" I asked, "Can that work?" I was really skeptical of this new idea I was hearing from Gary.

"If we can raise fish in the lake, we won't need to build cement fish tanks… We can raise more fish… Space won't be a problem anymore…," Gary said, as he continued to brainstorm.

"And," I joined in with the brainstorming, "You will be feeding all the other fish in the lake… You will have to catch your fish by going fishing… Your nets will be in everyone's way and they will break…"

"Why not submerge some kind of wire cages out in the lake to keep the fish together?" suggested Nancy.

"That's a good idea! Let's think through this and refine Nancy's idea," He suggested. Everyone got into the idea session.

"OK," someone said, "what if the cages were made out of steel mesh like Dave's chicken cages. Couldn't we build them quite a bit larger?

Maybe four-by-six feet and two feet high?" Another suggested.

"That's a good idea," Gary said, "If we built cages like that, we could have them partly submerged in the edge of the lake." He added.

"How would you get the fish in and out?" I asked.

"We'd have to figure a way to raise and lower the cage and use landing nets or something," he said. "Let's build a trial cage and try some things."

So during the next week we built two cages so the experiments would go faster. Next we filled the cages with fish. We submerged the cages so there was about a foot of water over and under the cage. We used floats and rock weights to keep the cages upright and in place. The problem came in feeding the fish.

"We need to redesign the feed so we're not wasting so much," Gary explained. "A lot of the feed dissolves too quickly, or falls through the cage and is lost or eaten by wild fish in the lake." We designed a feed pellet coated with the gum of a local tree so it would hold together in the water until the fish ate it.

"We need a way to make the feed hang buoyant three feet below the surface so it stays there until it is consumed," he suggested. We added an amount of finely ground coffee husk to the pellet to make the feed hang buoyant at precisely three feet.

"I think you've got it!" I said when we finally pulled off the first harvest of fish. "Now the biggest problem lies ahead."

"Teaching the villagers?" he asked.

"Teaching the villagers how to manufacture the feed correctly is the real work of this fish project," we both agreed.

Chapter 62

Moving Day

It was moving day!

A family in the neighborhood was moving to a different little wooden house about a block away. Lots of people showed up to help them move.

"OK... OK... Whoa!" shouted the man watching as Abram backed his little truck up near the house of the family who was moving.

They had their stuff setting everywhere outside and inside. Some was stuffed into baskets and some in boxes and other things were just piled here and there.

"Why did they mix things together every which way? Clothing thrown together with oranges and bottles and candles?" I wondered. "These things are strangely packed. Maybe they had too much help."

There were shelves and chairs and a table out in the yard near a pile of lumber, and about eight cement blocks piled up on top of some corrugated sheet steel used for roofing. Most of their stuff was loosely piled up here and there.

"Put those boxes of food and clothing in first," said the mother of the family that was moving. "Some of you can start moving that woodpile," she suggested to some neighbors who came to help.

They immediately formed a line and passed the firewood pieces one at a time down the line and into the truck, which was now also having the lumber passed towards the truck and thrown on top of the boxes and firewood pieces in the truckbox. They held up the loading for a moment as four men carried out a very heavy table and put that in the truck next.

"I think the truck is full," I said as I lifted a large box as high as I could reach, filling the top layer.

"We can get more on top of this stuff," said one of the women as she headed back into the house for more stuff. "Most of the boxes are already loaded. The baskets can go next, and then all the piles of loose things we'll put on top."

"But why?" I thought to myself. "Isn't it only like a block or so distance that we are going?"

They kept piling more things on. They had to load the chairs on the very top by gently throwing them up there, and having someone stand on the side of the truck bed, and reaching as high as he could, position them better so they wouldn't fall off.

They stopped loading the truck eventually only because they were out of stuff.

Abrams started the motor. Two men hopped up on either side of the truck box to help stabilize things. They would ride up there as sideguards. Abrams gunned the motor of his little Toyota truck.

He took off with the truck like a one-hundred-yard dash man comes out of the starting blocks. He was going thirty miles an hour by the time he had gone twenty feet. By the time he got to fifty or sixty miles an hour, it was time to begin pumping on the brakes so he wouldn't overshoot the house to which they were moving.

Things began to fall off almost immediately. Some things slid off the back when he lurched forward. I couldn't believe it. There were lots of people walking down the street to the other house to help unload. Everyone ended up carrying something. They carried the clothing, baskets, boxes, furniture, or other things that had fallen off.

"We were trying to save time," they would say if I asked, or, "We made it in one trip, which is always better than two trips, because it saves gas."

"But the family got moved," I thought, "and everyone helped them and that is important." Lots of their belongings got squashed or broken in the process...

But most of it was broken and tattered before we started.

Chapter 63

Women's Cannery

"The widows need work," everyone said. "There are almost five hundred widows in this village with young children to raise, and they all need an income!"

This condition was because of the continuing civil war that was going on. Everyone knew that, too. There were many meetings to get ideas of what these women could do to support themselves. Finally the widows themselves came up with a very good idea!

"Why don't we women have a canning factory," was the suggestion. It was quickly dismissed as impossible.

...But the idea lingered.

"We could can vegetables in little jars," one of them said.

"Yeah, great, and who would buy vegetables in little jars?" asked another woman, "Have any of us ever bought vegetables in little jars?"

"Perhaps we could sell them in the city or somewhere where people live, but don't have gardens or good open markets."

People began to perk up at these ideas. A vision for their "factory" was beginning to take form. It was fun to watch the tide of their hope go back and forth from positive to negative with each additional comment or idea. "Where would we buy the vegetables to put into the jars?" they were asking.

"The market is full of vegetables since the men began growing them down by the diesel pump," said one. "They are raising more than they can sell," said another. "A canning factory would help them with their sales," suggested a third. "The momentum was building... there arose a consensus among them that this was a good idea. They were all looking at me now.

"What?" I asked. They were looking at me for a comment now. They wanted me to make the decision. That way they could get out of making the decision in case it turned out bad.

They waited for my answer... "I know of a place in the city

where we can get a lot of jars," is all that I said.

"Put those tables in a long row over there," said one of the women. "Put them near the sinks." There were some men there too, building cooking stoves out of cement and stone. Things were beginning to take shape. It was the beginning of their little vegetable cannery factory.

"Where do you want me to unload these boxes of pint jars?" I asked the one who seemed to be managing things. They would soon have everything together. It would not be long before they would know how this project would materialize.

"We will begin the work next Tuesday morning!" it was announced

Twenty women would begin as workers. It was amazing to watch how the ones gifted with leadership, rose to positions of leadership. Those who could organize things were making plans, designs, and schedules for the factory operation. I liked their participation and involvement in making this thing work.

We met with the five leaders. "Light up one of the stoves," I announced. "First we must wash and scrub these carrots." Then we went through all of the steps of blanching the carrots, cutting them into proper pieces, making the brine, filling the six jars, getting the water boiling in the cooking kettle, sealing the jars, timing the cooking, handling the little pint jars, and finally cleaning and wiping them clean when they had cooled.

"This is a test run," we said. "Tomorrow is the first day with the workers here." You will be on your own to teach them and direct the operation. If it is not done properly, we cannot sell the product.

The six jars filled with diced carrots glistened on the table.

We were not able to return to the village for a week. When we returned, they had the three hundred pint jars that I had brought them all glistening and setting in rows on the tables. Chepe was taking them to the city to sell to the stores. It had taken twenty women three days of work to fill the jars.

"When we figured out the cost of the vegetables, the firewood, and the pint jars," said the one who became the accountant, "there is very little left over to pay ourselves any wages."

"What price did Chepe receive for the product?" I asked. It

was the price for which we had hoped. He had used part of the money for another three hundred jars.

"We are coming back tomorrow to begin again with the next batch," they said. "Come and see how well we work together."

"You are working very well together!" I said the next day as I watched them work. I was watching them work on the tomatoes beans and peas and carrots with my North American eyes though. First they all went to the sinks and washed and scrubbed the vegetables. Next they all worked on blanching them. Then all of them gathered around all of the tables and everybody worked at the same time to cut up everything. They all seemed to need to work on one task or the other all at the same time. "They work too well together," I thought.

It took three or four more sessions to get them to work in more of an assembly line production. It was an interesting process because they fought it every inch of the way. By the third session, they were actually doing it right, but none of them seemed to like it.

"This isn't how we work," they said. "We like doing things together because it's more fun."

"But this is more efficient," I argued, with full knowledge that I was going up against their cultural nature. "Why not work together in smaller teams on each phase of the production. There could be a scrubbing team, a cutting team, a cooking team, and so forth..."

The women, in charge of operations, called a business meeting of everyone. I figured that I was going to lose my battle for efficiency. They actually began by doing a production report in my favor. They were now producing six hundred jars in two days, they had said. Their working time was six times more valuable with my new working methods.

"We need to find more places to sell our products," suggested someone, "and we need some of us who are good at selling things, to go out and show our products to stores."

"We also need a better label for our jars!" said another.

I knew then that they were going to make it.

Chapter 64

A Tragic Gift

A twelve-year-old boy came into the large project office one morning and sat on a bench to wait his turn for assistance. He seemed agitated. He was perspiring. He also looked frightened.

"Hello," I said, sitting down on the space beside him. "You're here early this morning," I continued. His aspect seemed unusual.

"Yes," he said absently, "I'm here kind of early." He seemed to be a little distracted. He was actually squirming. Then I noticed that he was shaking as well as sweating.

"So…" I said. "How can I help, Antonio?" Then he suddenly became calm. He looked directly into my eyes for the first time. He seemed to be searching my face as if to make a decision. Then with much effort he slowly forced the words out…

"Two of my brothers are dead this morning," he said, holding back a great deal of emotion. He spoke quietly and slowly because his voice was shaky. "My cousin is dead, too," There were two loud sobs, then, holding it all back, he continued almost calmly…

"And my grandmother is unconscious and some men are taking her to the hospital."

"My God!" I said. I took his hands, which were shaking uncontrollably now, and called some others over to help me with this situation. "Antonio, this is horrible! What happened?" I knew his brothers and his grandmother well.

"I ran all the way here," he said. "I hollered for help when I couldn't wake them up this morning. Neighbors came to help and they said they thought they were all dead." He continued to tell of how he took off running when he saw them carry his grandmother out and put her into a car. They said they were going to take her to the hospital.

He said he ran and ran until he got to our office. He actually ran about three miles and through two other small villages to get here.

So… Bina and I went with Antonio. We drove the jeep to his house. There were people gathered everywhere.

"Come on, Antonio," I said as I rushed him through the crowd to where I had seen his mother. "We're very sorry about what happened!" I told her, taking her by the hands. "This is terrible." She told me how a neighbor had brought a charcoal burner to her three sons, the cousin, and her mother because the room where they were sleeping was cold. The charcoal warmed up the room nicely, but soon the glowing charcoal ate up the oxygen in the tightly-closed room, and they were all asphyxiated except for Antonio.

"It was an accident then," I said. "The good neighbor was being generous and trying to help."

"Yes," said the mother. "She is here," indicating the woman standing beside her. I learned later these two women were best friends since childhood. I reached out for her hand, repeating what I said about it being an unfortunate accident.

When something like this happens, everyone gathers together and wants to help, but there is nothing they can do. We are helpless, too. Everyone wants to comfort the family, but no one knows what to say to them.

"We are going to the village to get bread and other food for the crowd," we told her. We drove to two or three bakeries and bought all of their breads and put them in sacks and hauled them back to their house. The neighbors offered their kitchen for the food preparation.

"Lets get a couple of the big coffeemakers from the project house," said Bina. "They're going to need to make a lot of coffee." So we also picked up some coffee at the market, and a few bags of sugar. Then we drove back to the neighbor's house again. We had to make a third trip to buy a sack of black beans that we had forgotten.

They laid the bodies out on some tables; then, stretched a large piece of black plastic up on four poles to give some shade from the sun. "This is sad!" people were saying, "This is very sad."

There were rumors traveling through the crowd that the grandmother was better, then that she had died, and finally that she was critical. People came by all day long and offered to help.

They had some food and coffee and stood around awkwardly, not knowing what to say.

In late afternoon, they started the procession to the cemetery, carrying the little wooden caskets. They would carry them for the slow painful two-mile trip.

Then it was time for us to go back, too. "There is nothing we can do to help," we said, and silently drove the three miles back to the project house. I was rehearsing in my mind for the task I had yet to do…

I had three sponsoring godparents in the States to call with the sad news.

Chapter 65

Charcoal Market

"There is an elderly fellow with charcoal," said Abelino. "Let's ask him if he will sell some to us."

"OK," I said, as I drove the jeep over to the edge of the road. There was a man walking toward the market area with a large burlap bag of charcoal. With him was a helper carrying another bag.

"We'd like to buy some charcoal," said Abelino, to the older man with the load on his back.

The man looked surprised at us for a few seconds, then without a response put his bag down on the side of the road and began fiddling with the string, finally opening the twine with which it was tied. He opened the large bag and waited for us to say something…

"How much for a pound?" I asked.

The old charcoal man still had not spoken. He looked up at the first light streaks of the morning sky, and then he picked up some pieces of charcoal from the bag to show it to us. Then after an awkward moment we heard his voice for the first time.

"This is very good charcoal," was all he said.

"Yes, it's very good charcoal. How much per pound?" I repeated.

We knew that charcoal usually sells for eighty to ninety cents per pound. We needed a lot of charcoal and we were in a bit of a hurry to get back.

"How much per pound?" repeated Abelino.

"I think the going price is about a dollar per pound," answered the man, "because this is very good charcoal." There is a protocol to the way this market game is played. We were supposed to make a much lower offer. He was supposed to close up his bag and pretend to leave. Then we would make another offer. He would then lower his price a little and say it was his "final" price. Then it was our turn to walk away, at which time his "final" price got lowered. Then we would discuss the quality of the charcoal for a while...

That was "haggling." It was a ritual. It was the only way of selling something he knew of. We were supposed to finally agree on a price, knowing how many children he had to feed, and how far he had walked to the market.

"We'll take it," I said. He just looked at me as if to ask what that meant. "We'll take it for one dollar per pound."

There was disappointment on his face as he got out his balance scale and put the brass one-pound weight in one of the balance pans, and began to put pieces of charcoal into the other pan.

"No, wait," said Abelino. "We want to buy all of your charcoal. We want to buy both of your bags of charcoal."

The old man just looked at the large sack, then at the balance scale. Then he looked at his helper and his bag of charcoal. The helper was standing there the whole time with his bag still on his back frozen and listening to our conversation.

"We'll pay you your asking price for the charcoal," I said. "We'll pay you a dollar for every pound of charcoal you have." Then I added, "because it's very good charcoal."

"Yes," the man said slowly, thinking about our offer. "It's very good charcoal."

"So, how much for all of your charcoal?" asked Abelino.

"I can't sell you all of my charcoal," said the old man finally, "I can only sell you a pound or two."

"Why can't you sell all of your charcoal to us if we're willing to pay you your asking price for it?" asked Abelino.

The old man said nothing, but just wagged his forefinger from side to side, which means a definite "No." "There is something more than price going on here," I thought to myself.

"Do you plan to sell all of your charcoal at the market?" I asked.

"If I sell it all to you here," he explained, "I won't have anything to sell at the market."

"We'll save you the trouble of going to the market, if you sell it all to us here," we both said.

"No," he said. "Selling charcoal at the market is my work. If

I sell all of my charcoal now, I won't have work today."

"I'll weigh out two pounds for you," he said, and busied himself with his balance again, and we took the charcoal, paid him the money, and off they went with their loads, trudging towards the market place along the edge of the road.

Two blocks down the road we stopped and haggled some more. We bought two more pounds, this time paying only ninety cents per pound.

The old charcoal man made us go all the way to the market, and sit there and haggle for every piece of his charcoal pound by pound, until we bought all the charcoal in both of his bags. It took us more than an hour and a half.

This was the first anniversary of the opening of our school desk factory, which was really a carpentry school. We had invited all of the workers and everyone who lived in their houses with them. We had butchered chickens late the night before, and had two big tubs filled with cut-up chicken in ice water.

We were also doing an experiment. The blue tub had one kind of chicken in it and the red tub had another kind.

'What's the difference in the chicken?" the workers asked.

"We can't say," Pedro and I answered, "because that would influence your choice. We want to know which you like the best." Only Pedro and I knew what the difference was, and we weren't saying until all of the votes were in.

We built two long barbeque spits out of rows of cement blocks with welded cage wire stretched over the blocks. The space between the rows of blocks was for the charcoal. We had to make the barbeque sauce ourselves, which we put into several small pails. We bought small children's brooms at the market to put the sauce on the pieces of chicken as it cooked on our "grill."

"Remember which piece of chicken on your plate is from the red tub and which from the blue tub," announced Pedro over and over as people came for their two pieces of chicken.

"These are the desks we build," the men would say to their families, proud of their work. "And these are some wooden trucks we are beginning to build, too." The men had put up a display of some of their products.

They were giving their families tours of their workplace. We had maybe sixty or seventy people there counting the children. It was a good time and a great feast for everyone.

"The chicken in the blue tub won the taste test," Pedro said to me, after he had gone about asking everyone to give their opinion, "It won by almost all of the votes."

"So, what is the difference?" everyone asked.

"We dried a lot of onion and garlic and ground it into the feed for the last two weeks. The winning chicken in the blue tub got that 'onion and garlic feed.'" We explained.

"You seasoned the live chicken as they ate!" said one of the house-girls.

"We got the idea from the women who raise chickens in their patios," said Pedro, "and it worked."

That was our celebration. We sent the extra chicken home with the families along with the leftover charcoal.

Chapter 66

The Village Rooster

"When you think you've lost your way, it means you're probably on the right road. When you're sure that you're lost, you are almost there!" said the man giving us directions to a place called "Santa Maria."

He was right! It's a place high in the mountains; a place where not many visitors ever go. The road in is a real piece of work. It takes a good four-wheel drive and several hours to get up there. I don't think of it as a road... but rather a rough place winding upwards through the mountains where people drive to get there.

"This is where the church stood before the earthquake destroyed it," said one of the three men showing us their village. It was a beautiful pastoral spot. A few feet of crumbling and weathered adobe wall still stuck out of the grass here and there. The knoll where the church once stood was almost overgrown with grass now.

Some sheep were grazing there and a few lambs scampered about nearby. The view from there was breathtaking. One could see the peaceful fields spread out above the highland lake and two or three large volcanoes jutting skyward. Our house was down in the foothills of the largest of those volcanoes.

This was a small village, and many of the inhabitants had never seen the outside world. I was the only white skinned person many of the children had ever seen. Some of them touched my hands to see if my skin felt different from their darker colored skin.

These were honest, hard working people. They wanted to build a church, but the community was small and very poor.

"If we had the steel reinforcement rods and the cement we could get started," said the head of the community. The others nodded in agreement.

"So what do you do now for a church?" I asked.

"We use our own houses, but that's not very good," said another man. "We can't fit everyone into anyone's house."

"There is an old building still standing that we use once in awhile. We used it for community meetings before the earth-quake," ventured the third man. "But that building is not safe. Come, I'll show it to you." As we walked to that building, they explained that they didn't believe that God would let the building collapse if they were praying inside.

"God wouldn't let that happen," they said.

"This is dangerous!" I said immediately upon seeing the building, "These are adobe walls and the wood rafters are very poor. It wouldn't take much of a tremor to bring those heavy clay roofing tiles falling on everyone."

"There is a better building over there," said one of the men indicating with his finger farther up the road. "But it is smaller."

Every night they had something going on with their church. One night was for the women's groups, another for the Bible study, Wednesday nights were youth nights. The men's group got together to read scripture on Thursday evenings, and Friday night was rosary night.

On Sunday's they all got together to read the scriptures and do their Sunday prayer worship service.

"You folks really need to have a church building," I ventured. That was their problem.

That's why they came to see us. They needed help to figure it out and get a plan together. We did some measurements and got a consensus of their ideas. We wrote lots of their ideas in a notebook.

When we returned to Santa Maria on our next trip a couple of weeks later. We met with most of the townspeople to present what we thought would be a possible solution.

"We will look for a parish in the States who could donate all of the money necessary. There are many parishes that we know of that are also named Saint Mary's," I said.

"It would cost five thousand dollars for the benefactor's part of the building. That gift money would pay for the cement, re-rods, tools, hinges, paint, and other hardware and electrical supplies," I continued.

"Now for your part…" I said, and they all laughed.

"You will have to volunteer all of the labor." I began, "including cutting the timbers and lumber… And the lumber will have to be sawed out of the logs by hand!"

The list of the things they had to do was very long. It included mixing the cement, making cement blocks, cutting and forming rafters, making tiles for the roof. They also had to get sacks of gravel from the creek bottom below and haul them up to the church site, gather the large stone for making cement, and chipping volcanic rock into blocks to build doorways and steps and some of the walls and an altar.

"Remember, there is no guarantee that anyone would give you a five thousand dollar grant with this plan," I reminded them.

"No one will give us anything without a plan for sure," said the town leaders. And so they talked it over while we met more of the people and the women who had gathered too, and many of the children who were now out of school for the day.

"Yes," said the spokesperson later. "We've decided to commit ourselves to this plan of getting a church."

Then I went to my jeep and pulled out a package wrapped in burlap, and laid it on the hood of the jeep.

Everybody gathered around. I slowly unwrapped two large brass altar candelabras, each with holders for seven large candles.

The church that Betty had grown up in at Bluffton, Minnesota, had given these to us, and we thought it appropriate to give them to this community to mark a new beginning for them.

"There is one other thing we must do," I announced, "…and who can tell us what it is?" There was no need for an answer. They all knew.

They ran to pick flowers and put them in vases. They gathered up candles of similar sizes, and placed these large brass candelabras on the table, put the candles in the holders, lit them, and a prayer meeting was born.

It was a full house. People filled this smaller building, then gathered outside at both doorways on both sides. Some who wouldn't fit inside gathered outside of the large windows. The head of the community soon opened the Bible.

Later, as we were getting ready to leave, the people presented us with a very odd looking sack of something. I took the sack and realized that it was a live rooster. I pulled the rooster out of the bag and held it up for all to see.

They all applauded. When the rooster grabbed my hand and tried to fight me, they all applauded and laughed again. Then I stuffed him back in the bag and we left.

Receiving the prize rooster from the people of a village is the greatest of honors.

Chapter 67

The Lemon Harvest

There was a small village of about sixty families living on the land about two thousand feet below us on the mountain. These were good people and they struggled hard and I liked being around them.

"How are the orange groves looking?" I asked a group of the men one morning when I was there.

"They're getting ripe now and we're just beginning to truck the oranges to the city and sell them," said one of the men. "That gives most of the families here a little income," he added.

"What about the lemon trees?" I asked. "I was up there yesterday and no one is picking and selling lemons." We had planted the orange and lemon trees on community property and they belonged to the entire community to pick and sell.

"Not as many people buy the lemons because there is less demand," said another of the men. "People would rather sell oranges."

He was right. These were a very good variety of sweet seedless oranges that sold well and for a very good price. The lemons ripened at the same time, but went to waste because there was neither a good price nor a great demand.

"Let's drive up to the lemon grove and pick some," I suggested to my companion. So we drove the truck up the slow steady ten-minute climb where we had planted the citrus groves.

"Over there are some ripe oranges," said my companion as we passed through the rows of orange trees. "Let's stop and try an orange or two where those women are picking."

"Perfectly ripened," we said to the women picking nearby. A month ago another person in the orange grove taught me to peal and segment an orange in just a few seconds using my Swiss army knife.

"Show us how you do that," said one of the women. So I

pealed and segmented an orange in slow motion so she could see, handed her my Swiss army knife, then handed her a whole orange. "Wow," she said, "that's easy to do."

Above the large orange grove, we came upon the lemon grove of about three hundred lemon trees in full production.

No one was there picking the lemons.

"This is easy picking," said my companion, as we began picking and quickly filling the three sacks we had brought.

"Do you women want a ride down?" I shouted to five women who were heading back down with one-hundred pound sacks of oranges perched and balancing on their heads. We waited a few minutes for them to come walking out to the trail so we could hear their answer. It would take them about thirty or forty minutes to get to the houses down below on foot.

"It's difficult for us to get these big sacks back up and balanced on our heads," said one of them when they got to the truck. "When we arrive down below at the houses, will you promise to help us get the sacks back up on our heads again?"

When we said we would, they pitched their bags into the little truck almost like a soccer player bouncing the ball with their heads. The women just leaned their heads, pushing toward the spot where they wanted the bag to land in the truck bed.

"Hop in," we said after the truck bounced five times. The women climbed in and sat on top of their bags of oranges. It didn't take long for us to get down where the clusters of houses were.

"How can we put this heavy bag that weighs almost one hundred pounds on this poor woman's head?" I was thinking.

"Are you sure you can carry that heavy a load?" I asked them when we had lifted and perched the final bag on top of the head of the last one. They just laughed at my question. I didn't know any women who could do anything like that without collapsing.

And off they walked balancing their loads. Two of them carried their babies, too, and they all jabbered together as they walked along.

"Now we are going to squeeze these three bags of lemons," we announced when we got back up to our house

"Isn't that going to be a little more lemon juice than we usually use here at the house?" asked the house girls.

"We're not going to use this at the house here," I explained to them, "but we are going to squeeze the juice out so we can experiment." After a lot of squeezing, we put three gallons of the lemon juice into a large cooking pot on the stove.

"We have to cook this with a low heat until it gets as think as pancake syrup," I explained to them as they mumbled something about my being out of my mind, and they didn't think it would be any good at all on pancakes.

Hours later we were spreading the thick paste out on sheets of plastic so it could dry and get leathery. The next day we cut up the stuff and ground it like coarse hamburger to dry in the sun.

"Who's going to eat this stuff," one of them asked.

We used a coffee mill to grind our "lemon hamburger" into a very fine power.

"We're not going to eat it," I said. "We're going to drink it! We've been making instant lemonade." Then I put a large spoonful in a glass of water, added sugar, stirred it up, and took a sip. "You have to try it, it's great," I said finally.

"No, no, not us," they said, "we're just going to squeeze out a couple of lemons when we want lemonade. Your way of doing it is just too much work!"

Chapter 68

Family Moving Night

There is a joke about it being so dark that you can't see your face in front of you. I spent such a dark night with one family...

"It was a night when everything seemed impossible," I remember. "We ran out of everything... daylight, materials, time, and our faith almost..."

"We are running on empty," I said to Bina. We lacked inspiration and hope. In the darkness, the children and I carried the few pieces of old tin roofing, blackened from years of cooking over an open fire.

"Put those boards down over here closer to the fire," said Luis. "We'll have to pull those old nails so we can use them again."

We carried weathered boards and broken cardboard boxes of their stuff. There were rusty cans of rusty nails and wooden poles with the bark worn off. Bina was busy with the children packing things in boxes and sacks.

"Do you want this?" Marvin asked his dad, holding up a gunnysack with the bottom rotted out. Luis looked at the sack turning it over a couple of times to think if he could still use it somehow.

"Put it in the truck," he said finally. It took two trips with the pickup truck, but that was everything including more than a half dozen children, chickens, and pots and pans.

All of their possessions would bring five dollars at a garage sale...

"Silvia," I said, "you hold this pole here. Flower, you can hold this other pole like this," I said. "We're going to nail this piece of roofing tin to the poles, and then hoist it up." Flower's real name was "Magnolia," but I could never remember which flower, so I always just called her "Flower" instead, and that sort of became her name after that.

We placed the thin pieces of rusty tin on the flimsy poles for a roof. We nailed smaller pieces together to make walls and a corner with a roof on it where the family could sleep tonight

The entire family had three beds, one of them was only a child's size bed... and one had only cardboard between the children and the stretched wires. There were three or four worn and tattered blankets for all.

"We need to extend the roof farther," I said to Luis. "This is going to be too crowded."

"OK," he said, "let's use those last four sheets of tin. We can put that shorter piece at the end." It was very difficult working because it was almost too dark to drive nails, and the mosquitoes were bothering everyone.

One of the girls lit some cornstalks and put green weeds on them so the smoke would keep the night insects away. It was more difficult working in the smoke, but it gave us more light. After all, it was so dark you couldn't see your face... well anyway, by now a steady drizzle began, and drummed softly on our makeshift roof, and the nearby fire made it possible to straighten the old rusty nails before using them again.

This was the beginning point, the very dawn of development for them. We had learned that these children had not eaten all day, and yet, they could still smile. No one warned me about children like this.

"Do you have any corn dough left?" I asked. There was just a very little, so I built a small cooking fire, and soon the mother and one of the girls began to make a few tortillas.

It was one of those moments one remembers... the wood smoke, the pat-pat sound of making tortillas, the rain, the smell of children in wet clothes... I remember having an admiration for this family who just wouldn't give up. Then I realized that's why I wouldn't give up either...

It occurred to me that more food would be needed. So, Bina and I drove quickly to the project kitchen and raided the refrigerator of some of the food we found in a few bowls. We were back with the family in just a few minutes.

"Put some pieces of those short branches in this corner," I said to Marvin, the nine-year-old. There was an urgency in getting the boxes of their stuff out of the drizzle now, and under part of the roof.

"Put the cardboard boxes on the branches so they are off of the ground," I instructed the children who were carrying them, "and hold onto the bottoms so the box doesn't come apart!" I thought it would be best to put the boxes on some pieces of branches because the water might creep under the wall and get all of their clothes wet by morning.

Everyone was getting tired. We had been packing things up, taking their old house apart, moving their old house materials in the truck unloading the truck, rebuilding and getting things back together again. We were doing it all in the darkness and now in the dampening drizzle.

It seemed like there was no end to this struggle.

We were finally gathered together sitting under part of the roof and near enough to the fire for some warmth. We were rolling the hamburger we had brought from the project house into their tortillas. Bina was helping the younger ones with their food. We gave them the large plastic container of cooked pasta for tomorrow.

I recalled the faces of countless families who came before... struggling with patience and courage to rise from their poverty. It always seems to me that there is some kind of a holy presence or something, in people and conditions like these?

There was something very good and sacred about these people and their humble possessions, even in these circumstances. Perhaps there are many people who can remember a dark impossible night from which they refused to give up... And the unexpected help which finally came from far away...

They were tired, dry, and under a roof for the night when we finally left them and drove back to the project house.

The girls in the project kitchen always cook enough food on Saturday, so the volunteers have something to eat on Sunday when they are off.

"I thought the cooks were making some pasta and hamburger for us to eat today," said one of the volunteers the next day.

"It was here yesterday," said another. "Someone must have robbed our food right out of the refrigerator!"

"We can always eat eggs, toast, breakfast food, and peanut butter bread," I said. "But who would have the nerve to come and steal our food?" I asked, trying to maintain a level of concern in my voice.

Chapter 69

Maria Isn't Here

It's fun to go out to the villages and take photographs of the children because they get so excited and churned up. Some are nervous or reluctant, because they've never had their photograph taken before. The younger ones cling to their mother's dress and only peek out at us at first.

They are all freshly scrubbed and brushed and coached by their moms about how to sit properly and smile nicely. The little girls are all wearing pretty dresses, and the boys mostly wear button-down shirts and pants that some child in the community wore to first communion last year. Once in awhile their clothes actually fit.

We try to make it fun for them, too. We start out by trying to organize things, but when that gets to be a little like organizing bees, we just let things get chaotic and fun... and the children just keep buzzing and swarming around everywhere.

I chose a place on an adobe wall to take the photographs. It had crumbled for so many years, that now it was down to about two feet high There were some coffee trees hanging with ripe red coffee beans for an interesting background.

Picture-taking always goes well, but I think the moms and children never quite understand why they can't stand in the space behind the person having their picture taken.

So... someone had to keep chasing those bees out of the background.

We had a native worker taking down their names and birthdays in the order we took the pictures. Once we had two girls named Maria Hernandez from neighboring villages and they even had the same birthday. One wore a yellow dress and the other wore a red dress. I had to drive out to their houses to figure out which was which.

One little girl came up to have her picture taken, and I said, "I think we've already taken your picture."

"No you didn't," she answered.

"Yes we did... we took your picture about fifteen minutes ago," I responded.

"No you didn't," she insisted.

"I remember you... Are you Maria Zamora?" I asked her.

"Yes my name is Maria Zamora," she answered, "but you took a picture of my twin sister who looks just like me," she explained.

I turned to ask her mother who was with her, if she really named both of her twin daughters "Maria." I was asking out of curiosity, thinking that it was a crazy idea.

Looking steadily at me, she said, "That way I'll never get them mixed up!"

"So," I said, "we'll take her photograph now, but go and find the other twin and we'll take a picture of them together to send to whoever sponsors them." I knew quite a few look-a-like twins in the States who might like to sponsor twin look-a-like girls.

"No," said the mother, "you don't have to do that."

"Oh, but I want to," I said quickly, "and we'll make a copy for you to keep, too."

"No!" she said rather sternly, wagging her index finger side to side, "No!"

So I dropped the subject and went on with the picture taking. I've learned never to argue with the native women when they wag their finger side to side like that. I think herding bees would be more prosperous.

Anyway, we had a good time with the children and families. Sessions like that always seem to energize me. We said, "good-bye," and, "good wishes," many times and, "good health," and, "May God go with you," with many hugs to everyone.

Later as I drove the jeep back from the village, we talked about the photo session. I asked Rosa Elena, the native doctor who sat beside me, "Why wouldn't that mother let me take a photograph of her twin girls?" And I got a very strange look and a very surprising answer.

"Because," she said looking at me as though I were simple, "there may have been two girls, but they only had one dress!"

After I processed the photographs, I looked more closely and began discovering that each of the dresses in the photographs was worn by more than one or two little girls. I had discovered a new level of sharing unknown to those outside the world of poverty, where fine children's clothing is practically considered community property.

About a year later I was at the home of these twin girls. Only one of the twins was home. I was sitting on a woodpile in their yard talking with the one twin who was home, and her older cousin. As we talked we could hear the "slap, slap" sound of her mother and older sisters making tortillas in her outdoor kitchen not far off.

Suddenly her mother was in the doorway saying, "Maria, bring me some more firewood!"

"Maria isn't here, mama," Maria said loud and clear.

It served her mother right... naming them both "Maria" like that.

Chapter 70

Pink School Desks

Did you ever hear your little inner voice say things like, "This is none of your business," or perhaps, "You should get back to the project house because it's getting dark already." Well, I have a tradition of never, never listening to any such inner voice.

That's the voice I heard as I drove my little red jeep past some coffee trees and open areas on the outskirts of a large village. There was lots of dust in the air because of the dry season and the dirt road. The dust hung above the street glowing in the setting sun. I was actually in a bit of a hurry already, because I hadn't had much to eat since morning.

My eye caught a glimpse of something off to the right across an overgrown field. I stopped and backed up a half block to see if I could see what it was. I saw silhouettes of people moving about the sparkle of a small fire. That was enough for me. I drove my jeep to the side and headed off across that field.

That's when I heard that inner voice!

I first thought it was some sort of cook-out... then I realized it was just a very large family having their supper outdoors by this open fire. "Why not?" I thought. "I was hungry anyway."

When I arrived, I greeted the mother and father of the family, who were sitting on the ground together having a bowl of soup. After a couple of minutes, without invitation, I took a bowl and filled it with the ladle, and went to sit with them to eat with them. I had never met this family before. The mother seemed a little nervous.

When I took my first spoonful of soup, I learned why she was nervous. Then, without flinching or comment, I took another spoonful... then a third.

We began talking about their children and I heard their names for the first time. "This oldest one is 'Elizabeth,' that boy is 'Edi' and he is eight, and so on..." said the father. To me they seemed to be the smiling children of a happy family… and indeed they were.

The soup was made of grass and leaves torn into little pieces and cooked up in water. When I finished my first bowl, I got up and filled my bowl again because there seemed to be plenty. And the whole time we just sat there in the growing darkness and ate and talked. We never mentioned the contents of the "soup" we were eating. The children did not go to school because there was no money. There was no money because their father did not have work for a long time.

I explained about how we find sponsors so they could maybe send the oldest two children to school. Then I called Edi over and asked him if he would like to go to school and learn things. I asked him if he were smart and able to learn. I tested his math skills by giving him a little money and sent him running to the little store about four blocks away to buy three bags of noodles and bring back the correct change.

"Here, add one of these to the soup!" I said to Dominga, the mother, as I handed her the three bags of noodles. By this time the father and I were looking for the birth papers of those two oldest children.

They didn't exactly have a house. Instead they had a few poles that were tied together and covered with some blue colored sheet plastic. There was only crawling space inside. No one in the family could read or write, so I checked the papers in the firelight and they were correct, although in pretty much of a crumpled state.

The only food I found there was a half a carrot. Roberto said they were saving that.

"What do you do," I asked Dominga, "when your children get really hungry?"

"We take them down to the water tank and have them drink as much water as they can so their stomachs don't hurt," she said. "That way they can at least sleep."

The next morning, Roberto showed up at our house like we had arranged. I gave him some boards and tools and nails and glue and things like that to build each of his children a school desk. That way they wouldn't have to sit on the cement floor, because I knew there were no extra desks at the school in that village.

So we had a plan. He and the two children began measuring and sawing and sanding and nailing until they had constructed a couple of rather interesting school desks. Then I showed him where we kept the paint and told him to pick out a color, mix the paint well, and paint the desks, too.

He painted them bright pink!

He had not gone to school himself, so he didn't know that pink was an unusual color for school desks. The inside of a school remained a mystery to him. But, there would never be any mistaking these two pink school desks, however, and to whom they belonged.

Chapter 71

Christmas Rejection

This story is like the Christmas story of Mary and Joseph and their arrival in Bethlehem when they were searching for a place to stay.

It never occurred to me to think about the look on Mary's face each time they were rejected, or consider how powerless Joseph felt inside when there didn't seem to be anywhere else to go. This is the story of how I discovered what it must have been like for them.

"I think that woman down the street is waving to me," I thought. "Yes, she is waving!" I was in an outback village and it had pretty bad streets. I turned my jeep down her street, finally arriving at the place where she was.

"My baby," she was saying, "my baby is very sick! Can you help me?"

I got out of the jeep and looked at the child she carried on her back. "This child needs to see a doctor," I said, placing my hand on the child's face. The child was burning up with fever.

"What can be done?" she asked. "The child is very ill."

"I will take you to the larger village nearby where there are several clinics with doctors," I suggested. "Come on, I'll help you in the other door of the jeep."

"Gregorio!" she shouted towards the nearby house. "My husband will come along to help," she said to me.

In a short time we came to the first clinic where we were turned away. The receptionist called the doctor who took one look at the child. They shook their heads negatively.

It's a problem when they do not think the child will make it...

Most are amiable about it... advising other places to go. On one street I brought the medic right out to the jeep. When he refused to offer help, I saw clearly the look in the mother's eyes. I could sense her struggle not to lose hope.

"Come back in the morning," said one medic. But these parents knew that without help, the child would not see another morning. It is the doctor's way of doing nothing without saying, "no."

"When they look at us," said Gregorio, "they know that we cannot pay. They can see that we are poor."

Down the street a nurse stepped halfway out of a door to see... then closed the door again without a word. The mother looked painfully at the closed door for a moment as her husband looked blankly at the dirt street avoiding her eyes.

The problem was that these were the very poorest of us, and there was little chance for the child to survive. It might hurt someone's reputation to lose a patient. The parent's desperation was familiar, but now I could never forget this new look...

...The pain of total rejection in a mother's eyes.

We eventually made the two-hour drive to a distant hospital where they always take our children. I stayed with them until the child was safely responding. Like the story of Mary and Joseph, this story ends happily, but many similar stories do not.

When Jesus said, "Whoever welcomes one of these little ones, welcomes me," I often wondered if Jesus had in mind the story Mary must have told him of his own birth.

...A story of desperation and rejection, having been born into conditions of poverty himself.

Chapter 72

Chicken Entrepreneur

"It feels like we could tip over, doesn't it?" I asked Jim as we drove with one tire up on the aqueduct and the other down in the muddy earth. It was tough going through the low brush, too, because we couldn't see steadily with all of those branches scraping over the truck.

The look on Jim's face was answer enough. His half of the truck was up several feet higher than mine. "Remember, Jim," I said laughing, "you're in charge of your half of the truck!"

"Are you sure you want to be driving here?" asked Jim now in earnest, rather surprised by the situation in which we found ourselves.

"Of course," I answered. "We wouldn't want to be walking through this crap, would we?" I was trying to relieve the tension. Then suddenly, like driving out of a thick fog, we could actually see where we were going a lot better.

"There he is over there," said Jim, indicating where Luis was going ahead of us trying to lead us through the thickest part. Then the going got better, although the truck was still going with one side up and the other side down. It was fun to watch Luis now. He was running backwards, motioning for us to keep coming.

"He is excited about getting these chickens," said Jim laughing at the way he was guiding the truck forward, motioning this way an inch and then that way.

"He doesn't know how to guide the truck because he doesn't know how to drive," I said. We had just driven between two trees that we shouldn't have fit between. "From here it is clear sailing," I announced.

"Until we have to drive back out!" stated Jim. We were both hopeful that there would be another way back.

"I think it's the only way out," I said.

"So, Luis," I began, "where are the chickens you're supposed to be getting?"

"In that shed over there, I think," he said. Then he went to another building and knocked at the door. A man answered and they talked for a bit, before directing us with the truck to back up to a different faded red building.

We spent the next half hour catching and sacking chickens. These were laying hens that Luis was buying that had been culled out. They were culled out and being sold because they had stopped producing eggs.

We weighed every sack, added it all up, got a total and I paid the man for his chickens. This would be a start-up loan for Luis's new chicken business.

"OK," I said, "we're finished." It was already getting dark so we had to get going. "Ride inside, Luis!" I shouted, and he got in the passenger side of the truck, and we headed for the same road out. This time we drove in the dark, and my side of the truck was up on the aqueduct, and Jim's side was down in the mud.

Luis was going into business. Jim was a very good business-man, and he went over the plan and the numbers pretty carefully. Luis understood very little about business and profits and margins.

"Jim and I went over the numbers pretty carefully," I said to Luis, who had little education or practical experience. "You can make some money if you figure it out right," I said.

"You know how many pounds you bought and what you have to sell it for, don't you?" we asked him.

"I can figure it out," Luis had told me, "so that we can make a good profit." At some point one needs to let the person receiving help take over the whole show, like letting a child take their first steps.

The idea of his business was to sell fresh dressed chicken at their door. They had a scale and could weigh each sale and sell whatever pounds anyone wanted. They could sell one piece or as many pieces as anyone wanted. To protect our investment we agreed that all sales would be for cash with no "pay-you-tomor-row" credit sales.

"Come over and check things out," said Luis a few days later. "We don't seem to be taking in as much money as we should be."

"Luis, there is a problem," I said after going over their system. "You are buying live chickens, and selling dressed chickens."

"I know that, but what is wrong about the money?" he asked.

"When you dress out a live chicken," I explained, "you're throwing away the feathers, the guts, the feet, and the blood. After the chicken is dressed out, the chicken weighs a lot less than it did before, right?" He still didn't get it.

"You buy a five-pound chicken for five dollars, OK," I said.

"OK," he said.

"You only get to sell a three-and-a-half pound chicken now because you dressed it out, OK," I said.

'OK," he said slowly, his eyes moving around like the thoughts moving around in his head.

"How much do you sell the chicken for?" I asked

"We paid a dollar per pound, so I sell the chicken for a dollar and a quarter per pound." He answered.

"How much does the chicken you are selling weigh, again?" I asked.

"Three and a half pounds," he answered.

"Well, there you have it!" I said, "Three and a half pounds of chicken multiplied times your 'dollar and a quarter' is only four dollars and thirty-seven cents. You paid five dollars for it!"

"Are you telling me that every time I sell pieces of chicken, I'm losing money?" he asked, putting his hands on his head, "and the more chicken I sell, the more money I lose?"

"I'm afraid so, Luis, but at least you have good market share!" I said. He seemed to agree, although I know he didn't understand what "market share" meant. "We'll fix the problem tomorrow morning, Luis. We'll adjust the sale price of the chicken so that you are making both good sales and good profits."

"I've got it figured out," he said the next morning. "We're going to charge a dollar and ninety cents per pound."

"OK, Luis, but let me know when you run another special!" I said.

Chapter 73

Mountain Jeep Ride

A woman from back home came to visit for a week or so. She was one of those hardy people who could handle adverse living conditions and rugged terrain. "You're a real trooper," I'd say to her.

She was well able to keep up out in the villages, too. One day we went to visit the site of a new school construction. We were still in the excavation phase, digging up the earth looking for volcanic rock to use as building materials. We went there because her financial gift in memory of her husband, helped get this school started.

"It's a mess!" I said to her. There were deep holes and piles of rock and stone and gravel everywhere. Men were there hammering with chisels breaking up the larger boulders.

I introduced her to these workmen from that community. They insisted on taking a photograph with her in the middle of all of them, hammers and chisels in hand.

That photograph of her is probably hanging there in that school today.

On our drive back through that same village later in the day, the men from that community stopped us to present her with a beautiful hand-woven tablecloth. It was a weaving made by several women of that community.

So then... off we went. "Should we take the scenic route?" I asked, pointing to a road much higher on the mountain.

"Yes!" she said, "why not?" At first she liked it until we got much, much higher and the road got much, much narrower. The turns were sharper with sheer drops to the left and the mountain wall to the right. I never could figure out how they could even build a road in an impossible place like that.

We could see birds flying far below us.

I had an altimeter installed in the jeep, which she watched until the needle finally reached over nine thousand feet. I suppose

I shouldn't have started talking about earthquakes at a time like that, and drivers getting dizzy and passing out in the thin air, but I wanted it to be a ride she did not soon forget.

"Why did they build a wall across the road here?" she asked at one point.

"Oh," I said, "that's not a wall, that's what the road looks like when it goes upward," and we started to climb, climb, and all we could see was sky out of the windshield. I think she remained in constant prayer until we got back down to the flatter area.

I did get her to say it was an interesting ride, although her knuckles turned a little white as we came down the other side. I think she would have gladly given away her tablecloth to be on a level road somewhere else just then. That's when I said it...

"You're a real trooper," I said, and she really was.

Chapter 74

A Grandmother's Legacy

"Who is that old woman named Beata who lives in that tiny village on the mountainside above Santa Ana?" I asked.

"She is a good old woman, and now quite up in years," the ladies washing clothes answered. "And she had always lived up there." The tiny village in which she lived was stuck up on the side of the mountain. The paths of the village were laid out directly uphill or downhill, crossing and zigzagging and winding around impossible climbs and descents.

"She is my grandmother," said one of them.

"And everyone else's," said the other two laughing. "Almost anyone under thirty who lives around here, calls her grandma. Almost nobody calls her Beata anymore, just grandma."

The villagers were all squatters living on the most marginal government land. This old woman was able to travel about, only with great difficulty because of the incline. She was a gentle, humble woman who would often sit and tell stories of long ago to the children.

Once at Christmas my son, John, and I climbed up to that village and spent part of the afternoon bringing each family a Christmas gift basket. Each basket contained a chicken and other food for their Christmas dinners. We walked around delivering the baskets to the families who lived there.

"I think I'll give the old woman this basket," said John, noticing her on a path half hidden behind a fence and hedgerow. "I'm going over to that gate to get through to the other side of this hedgerow." When she saw him head for the gate, however, she began to leave on the far side.

"We want to give you this basket," John shouted to her, but she was shy, and there was no coaxing her to either come out to us, or to stay there as we came to her.

"I think she wants to have the basket," I said, "but she is too shy to come out here where we are."

"I have an idea," said John, and he took the basket to a thicker part of the fence hedgerow near where she was. "I'm going to stick the basket through the fence so she can see it, then I'll just hold it there for her."

She was then able to clearly see the basket from the other side.

After a minute and without a word John slowly felt her hands taking the basket as he gently let go. John's determination overcame her resistance.

She would have her Christmas dinner after all.

More than a year passed, during which we had gradually come to know her and the families in that area better. One evening one of her grandsons came to tell us that his grandma was very sick and was unable to walk down to our clinic.

"Maybe a couple of us can go up to see her," I suggested, thinking that maybe we could walk down with her, and drive her most of the way with the jeep.

"She is not very good," observed Pedro privately, when we finally got up to where she lived.

"We can't bring her down in her condition," I said quietly to him. "But let's talk to her for awhile. Maybe we can figure out if there is anything we can go and get for her." We learned that she had been sick for quite a number of days, and hadn't wanted to eat much of anything.

So we talked with her for a long time. "Are you in any pain?" I asked.

"Some pain, but not much," she said in a very weak voice. "Mostly I feel weak and uncomfortable," she added. Then we stayed with her and talked for about an hour. It had already grown quite dark by then, so Pedro lit a lantern that was there in the room. By the end of the second hour, we both could tell that she was getting much weaker.

"Do you want to pray?" I asked her, knowing that her faith tradition was evangelical, and she would probably want to pray.

"Yes," she said, as she squeezed my hand and nodded her head affirmatively. So we began, beginning with the "Our Father" and other praying that we just spoke from the heart. "I feel strange... like I might be dying," she said to us after a while. She had to say it twice for us to understand what she was saying.

"Pedro, go tell her daughter and family in the other houses to come now," I said. Then Pedro went out to find her daughter and more of her family. Some family members came, but most of them seemed uncomfortable and didn't stay long.

Then we talked and prayed for a while longer, as she lay there quite peacefully. Suddenly she began to speak in a low quiet manner. I had to get my ear close to understand her. I looked at Pedro, who shrugged his shoulders as if to ask, "What is she saying?" She continued to speak and I continued to listen with my ear close. Suddenly I became aware of what she was saying.

"She is talking about her sins," I realized. "She is saying what she has done in her life that was wrong. She was going to confession... confessing her sins in preparation for her death." Then, when she finished, she looked at me intently and in great earnest.

"I believe that Jesus has forgiven your sins," I told her. "He has died for us on the cross for our sins. You believe that don't you?" I asked.

A weak smile was her answer. Then we prayed some more, but before we finished, she was gone... and somehow we just knew that she was in a very happy place.

Some neighbors and family members carried her down from her mountain home the next day. It was a difficult task because of the steep incline of the pathway.

As we were descending from her place on the mountain, I noticed one of the women of the family was carrying the woven wicker basket that John passed over to her through the hedgerow to brighten one of her Christmases.

"Why do you carry her basket down?" I asked quietly.

"This basket and what it contains, are all of her worldly possessions," she answered, "and we will give each person something today by which they can remember her."

And then later we laid her gently in the earth.

Chapter 75

The Inspired Roofers

Enthusiasm can get really contagious. I saw it happen to a group of men in one of the communities where we were building a school.

The story actually begins very early one Friday morning as I and a group of about a dozen visiting college students were busy loading a couple of trucks with lumber and tools. The college students were with us for a "January Term" from Saint John's University, The College of Saint Benedict, and Saint Thomas College.

We were preparing to make the journey to a school-building site in a village across the mountains. There we would build the school desks the children will need when their new school building is finished. The travel by trucks through the mountains to the school site took about an hour.

"The area near the school is too close to the mountainside to work there," I said to the group, "so, let's work in that field over there where the land is flat.

"Unload the radial arm saw and generator on that grassy place," said the student placed in charge of that work, "and put the lumber on the other side of the saw so it will be handy," he added.

"The desks will be long benches to hold three students each," said one of the college women as she explained the design of the school desks to a group of others. Then she passed out papers with the plans and dimensions for them to study. They were all ready to begin!

"Start the generator!" said someone getting ready to begin sawing lumber.

It was amazing! Everyone seemed to know what to do. It was like clockwork to watch them organize into a "desk-building" assembly line. Henry Ford would have been proud! Soon the people of the community came to help.

They were drilling, nailing, sawing, and putting in screws. The women of the community were sanding and putting on the wood sealer. The children were carrying things, and playing with the little blocks of wood falling from the saw, and often touching the sticky desks that had fresh sealer applied to them.

It would take about four hours to complete the job. We had a mighty crew! I think it might have been the buzz of the generator or the wailing of the radial arm saw that helped peak everyone's energy.

Suddenly I noticed a very strange thing happening. All of the men of the community left. The women and children stayed, but all of the men had quit.

"Did anyone say anything to upset them?" I wondered...

But we kept going, and going, and going... And in a few hours we had the end in sight. I knew that we would all be wiped out when we got back home across the mountain. It would be a good day that we would all remember... except for all of the men who left early.

"Let's carry the desks over to the school now," I suggested. So everybody carried desks. "We must look like worker ants carrying everything to a new location," I thought, as we followed each other, each group with a desk, in a winding line leading over to the school.

A surprise was waiting there for us!

The men had gotten so caught-up in our enthusiasm, that they decided to go into the mountain and cut the rafters and carry them down, hue them out, raise them up into place, nail the corrugated roofing steel into place, and completely finish roofing the new school!

School opened on Monday morning! It was the first school opening ever for this community.

Chapter 76
The Photographer

Sometimes when I need to travel to the States, things get very busy just before the day of my flight. I usually have to pack late in the night before my early morning departure.

There are too many things to take care of... Too many things to prepare... instructions to give... people to see... I have separate lists for the office, the villages, the volunteers, and a "whatever" list. That's before things begin to break down. "When did that tire go flat on the jeep?" I'd ask.

"By the way," I would hear, "the jeep's spare is flat, too."

I got a visitor. "I don't have time now for a visitor," I thought, as I welcomed him in and took some time to visit with him. It was an offer to help wherever we needed someone. He didn't speak Spanish. He didn't know where the villages were. He couldn't drive in this country. He only had two or three days until his plane left, too.

"There are only three days left, and I need a week," I thought. "There must be something on my list for him to do!" If he could do something on my list... that would really be good. I looked over my lists, but found nothing there that I could ask him to do.

"I've got lots to do," I said as I looked over my lists again. "I could use some help," I confessed, "because I'm leaving for Minnesota on the same day you are flying out. For most of the things on my list you need Spanish, or you need to know where things are."

I was remembering a sign I'd seen in a mechanic's shop in my hometown in Minnesota: "Labor is twenty dollars per hour, if you help it's twenty-five dollars per hour." Most of the things on my lists were like that.

"There is only one thing on my list that I might ask you to do," I began. "It's not really working together with people, and you will have to go out and do it on your own."

"What is it?" he asked curiously. "Tell me, maybe I'll like

it."

"I'm embarrassed to tell you," I said. "But I have a list of photographs that I need taken before I leave. I have this old 35mm camera that you can use and a half dozen rolls of film."

"I can try that," he said. I explained about the light meter and the camera settings, and how to load the film... He seemed pleased and smiled at this new challenge. Then I went over the list. A man carrying wood, a woman washing clothes at the public tank, children in a classroom, men hoeing their corn, women carrying water jugs on their heads, mothers with babies, houses, etc.

Then he asked, "Can I use my own camera that I brought down with me?"

"Sure, if you want to," I answered, thinking he would be able to understand his own camera better than my strange one.

Then he left. He seemed pretty happy. I was still a little embarrassed at asking him to do that, instead of something more interesting with some human interaction.

I didn't see him again until the afternoon before the day of my departure. Suddenly, he bounced in with his backpack. He then reached into his backpack and pulled out the most beautiful photographs. He had photographs of all of the things on my list. They were outrageously good.

"These are great!" I said. "How did you do this?" I asked as I picked the photographs from the table one after the other. "Each one is beautiful! These are perfect!" He seemed pleased that I liked them.

"You ought to be a photographer!" I said. "You've got a lot of talent!"

"I am," he said with a smile. "I'm a photographer for the *Washington Post*."

Chapter 77

The Man with Ten Cages

"I want to learn to raise chickens," said Carlos, after looking at some of our cages filled with different ages of chickens at our growing operation at San Lucas.

"Where do you live?" I asked. "Are you here in the village or do you live down the mountain?"

"I live down the mountain at the entrance to the San Martin farm," he responded. "We are in the cluster of houses on the left."

"Would tomorrow be a good day for us to stop by at your house?" I asked. We've learned that it's always best to make a visit before we commit to a chicken growing project for anyone.

Carlos lived in a small house with a larger than normal yard. There would be space for him to begin a chicken-raising program. He had lots of children to help with it. He worked on the nearby San Martin Farm. In one part of his back yard he had a tiny corral with two of the sickliest, thinnest, and scrawniest pigs I have ever seen. "These hogs are so thin," I thought to myself, "that they'd have to walk past twice to make a shadow."

"You have the space for growing chickens," I told him right away. "The problem is that most of the money we've allocated for chicken growing is for widows who have dependent children."

"Why don't you just tell me all about raising chickens, and I'll try to do it on my own?" Carlos suggested. He really wanted to raise chickens.

The real problem was that he had those hogs there, and I knew what would happen. Everything would start out great, then after a while he'd start stealing corn from his chickens and give it to his runty pigs. He would have to feed pigs like this for years and it would be like throwing away money because they would not grow. They were runts. One of them weighed about one hundred twenty pounds and the other about sixty-five pounds.

He didn't want to sell the runty hogs. I couldn't waste my

time and resources on chickens that were doomed to fail because of those hogs. Then I got an idea.

"There is a way for us to do a chicken project for you," I said. "We can provide you with a cage and all of the start-up things you need, including the baby chicks."

"I thought there wasn't enough money for that," he began.

"I'm coming to that part of the deal," I said. "You will have to give me sixty-five dollars cash to begin. If you can raise five groups of chickens at a profit, I will give you the cage and all of the equipment to continue... and I will also give you all of your sixty-five dollars back."

"That sounds like a good deal to me," said Carlos. "But I don't have sixty-five dollars to get it started."

"Then we can't do it," I said. "Let's give it some time and maybe we'll think of another idea, unless you can come up with sixty-five dollars." Then we shook hands and I left.

A week later he was at my door. "I still haven't any ideas about how I can get the money to raise chickens," he related. "Isn't there some way that you can loan me the money, being you will be giving it all back to me later anyway?"

"Sorry, Carlos," I said. "There just doesn't seem to be another way that I can do it."

More than a week passed before I saw Carlos again. "I got an idea," he told me. "I have the money." He reached into his pocket and pulled out some bills and counted out the sixty-five dollars into my hand.

"Well, we're in the chicken business!" I said. "Lets get started." So we got started that very day. When we set up the cage in his yard there wasn't a pig to be seen. He had gotten the price for them that I had predicted. In two months he was showing a nice profit already on the chickens.

"You're expanding," I said as I pulled in his yard, and saw a second cage there filled with chickens, too. He and his two sons were already building a third cage. He got so good at building cages out of bamboo, that he began selling cages.

"I'm going after the markets now," he told me on one visit. "I'm taking orders for 'fresh dressed' chicken in a few restaurants on the coast. I deliver it to them ready to cook." Carlos had been on his own now for quite awhile. The last time I visited, he had ten cages lined up on his property with chickens of every age so he always had a product ready for his growing customer list.

One afternoon I had a group of about twenty people on a grassy hillside where I was introducing my economic cage system of growing chickens. We were beginning to talk about feed mixing and protein...

Suddenly Carlos drove up with a pickup truck. "Hello, Carlos!" I said. "Can I interest you in raising a couple of skinny hogs? They'll only cost you about sixty-five dollars," I laughed.

"I figured out a long time ago how you got me to sell those old pigs," said Carlos. "You did me a very big favor!"

"I came to talk to your group here," he said to my surprise.

"Go ahead," I said, motioning him to step forward. Carlos was now no longer part of the problem; he was part of the solution. He spoke to my group telling his chicken-raising story and his expansion and marketing.

"I was able to go out and buy that pickup truck," he told my group. "I never thought I could own a pickup, but now it's just another tool in my business." Then he pointed to the beautiful bamboo cage in the back of his truck.

"Whoever makes the most profit on your first cage of chickens, will get this cage that I have built."

I knew by his joy in giving this gift, that Carlos had discovered something beautiful about the meaning of life... "The meaning of life is discovering one's gifts, and the purpose of life is giving them away."

Chapter 78

God Will Repay You

There is a beautiful traditional blessing: "God will repay you." These are words often spoken by the parents or children as they receive the help and assistance given them. Volunteer workers actually hear these words many times every day... They are spoken so often that after a time one could easily miss their impact.

The real meaning of this blessing is profound. The poor know that the help that they receive is far beyond their ordinary means. They would never be able to repay so great a gift. It is always much more than they expect. It is always their means of hope for tomorrow.

"Felipe, get your school notebook and a pencil," said the father of one of the families we had worked with for some time.

"Sit down, Felipe. You are going to write a letter for me," continued his father. "You have learned to write, so I will tell you the words to put down." The father could neither read nor write, and so had his son write the letter to me.

After dictating the letter, he rubbed some ink on his thumb, and made a thumbprint on the paper where a person would usually sign it. "Now write my name around my thumbprint," he said to his son.

He walked three miles to bring the letter to me the next day. It was a humble and sincere letter, which said at some length, "thank you for saving the life of my wife, and one of my little girls. We would have lost them both without your help." He also said, "God will repay you!"

It was a wonderful letter to receive. Although this smudgy letter was written on paper torn from an old notebook, it was not possible to return a gift to him of equal value. It was a privilege to accept this humble and sincere blessing from the poorest man I knew, who gave me the best of all blessings!

An afterword

Abelino Tun is a carpenter and operates his own custom furniture establishment in San Lucas. (Chap 15, 65)

Ana Vasquez, Pedro's wife, presently works at *Common Hope* in an administrative capacity. (Chap17, 19, 48)

Annie Huebsch operates a photographic studio, *Annie Marie Photography*, 350 Water St., Excelsior, Minnesota, specializing in children and graduate photography. (Chap 17, 50)

Betty Huebsch, Dave's wife of 31 years and co-founder of *Common Hope*, died suddenly of an aneurysm in December 1989. (Chap 2, 17, 20, 24, 66)

Bina Huebsch, a nurse married to Dave Huebsch in 1996, is co-founder of *Rising Villages* which presently gives retreats in Guatemala. (Chap 64, 68)

Dave Huebsch Jr, lives in Oceola WI, and works as a family counselor. (Chap 17)

John Huebsch is presently the Executive Director of *Common Hope*. (Chap 10, 17, 74)

Monica Cos is presently married and is raising a family in San Lucas. (Chap 23, 35, 48, 50)

Pedro Julajuc, Dave's godchild and Ana's husband, died on a mountain curve accident in 1993. (Chap 29, 33, 37, 47, 50, 59, 65, 74)

Sister Maria Mahia, a Guatemalan Franciscan Sister, became foundress of her own Nutrition Center and Clinic. (Chap 54, 56)

Common Hope

FAMILY DEVELOPMENT IN GUATEMALA

Common Hope is an organization dedicated to bringing help and hope to desperately poor families in Guatemala by empowering them to permanently lift themselves out of poverty, while keeping their dignity and independence. *Common Hope* was founded in 1986 to work in education, health care, and family development.

Since then, *Common Hope* has grown from a small family-based project to a powerful force helping families rise from poverty. The families who walk through *Common Hope*'s doors are often barefoot, live in one-room dirt floor shacks made of cornstalks, and have little access to medical care, clean water, basic sanitation, education, or jobs.

Common Hope today is made up of many volunteers who work in numerous villages in several parts of Guatemala. They also host medical and construction teams from the United States.

Common Hope is non-political. Its vision and philosophy are based on Christian principles. It is non-denominational and does not proselytize.

Common Hope
PO Box 14298
St Paul MN 55114
Phone: 651-917-0917
info@mn.commonhope.org
www.CommonHope.org

Give the gift of *Village Assignment* to your friends.

☐ Yes, I want _____ copies of *Village Assignment* for $16.95 each.

☐ Yes, I am interested in having Dave Huebsch speak to our church, service club, or civic organization. Please send particulars or call.

Free shipping and handling for all orders in the Continental United States or Canada. Minnesota residents add 6.5% sales tax ($1.10/book). Payment must accompany order. Allow three weeks for delivery.

My check or money order for $_____is enclosed.
Please charge my ☐ Visa ☐ Mastercard

Name _____

Organization _____

Address _____

City/State/Zip _____

Phone (_____) _____ - _____

Card # _____

Exp. Date _____

Signature _____

(10% of all book sales are contributed to volunteer organizations serving the poor in Guatemala's villages.)

(for same day shipping)
Call toll free: (866) 336-6681 *(have card # ready)*
Make checks payable and return to

Highlight Publishing
PO Box 27
Little Falls MN 56345
www.HighlightPublishing.com